HAMLET
(IN REHEARSAL)

Donald Freed

I0140296

Preface by
Alistair Stead

BROADWAY PLAY PUBLISHING INC
New York
www.broadwayplaypublishing.com
info@broadwayplaypublishing.com

HAMLET (IN REHEARSAL)
© Copyright 2008 by Donald Freed

Cover art by Rebecca Keating

First printing: December 2008
This edition: April 2018
I S B N: 978-0-88145-400-0

Book design: Marie Donovan
Word processing: Microsoft Word
Typographic controls: Ventura Publisher
Typeface: Palatino

Giving Hamlet the Ghost of a Chance: Donald Freed's New Thought Experiment

"Who's there?" Well, in the autumn of 2007 I am in privileged attendance at the try-out of Donald Freed's remarkable revisiting of Shakespeare's tragic masterpiece in the Studio of York Theatre Royal, York, England. It is a spirited and moving production. Although it understandably lacks some of the technical magic demanded by the imaginative script published here—"The Ghost's Special" and the subtle poetic lighting of the great final scene—the performance of the play (in draft) by a talented cast of students is being overseen by the dramatist himself. Yes, Donald Freed is also here as an inspiring guest artist at the York Theatre Royal (2007-2008). He is the prolific American playwright and novelist, a sorely-tried political dissident, still best known perhaps for his co-authorship of Secret Honor, that fine play about President Nixon which Robert Altman filmed in perhaps the best of his remarkable stage-to-screen adaptations, but Freed ought to be better known for decades of distinguished experiments in radical theatre. Shamefully, only a handful of these have been produced in the U K, among them, CIRCE AND BRAVO, VETERANS DAY, THE DEVIL'S ADVOCATE, and, most recently, PATIENT NO.1, a provocative fantasy about a post-Presidential and instutionalised George W Bush, given in a first-rate production by York's Damian Cruden.

I have chosen to open this introductory essay by quoting the question which thrillingly opens the

famously enigmatic tragedy and which is quoted in
Act One of the partial text of Hamlet which is being
rehearsed in Freed's play. The original ambiguity of
the sentry's nervous challenge—does it express his
fear of an encounter with an enemy of the state, or of
a ghost?—offers an instance of what undergirds Freed's
ingenious re-interpretation of Shakespeare's most
celebrated work: equivocation, haunting, and the
looming shadow of a dangerously fearful state.
First, equivocation, since it is basic to this playful new
version's strategy, building on traditional observations
on the equivocal natures of the ghost and the hero's
madness. The sentry's words are already equivocal:
of doubtful meaning, capable of more than one reading
or hearing. But then, repeated in rehearsal, and
afterwards in public performances, all the words of the
dramatic text are susceptible to another interpretation.
As the great sixteenth-century essayist Montaigne
whom Shakespeare read writes, in Florio's translation, "
Words reported again have as another sound, so
another sense". The contemporary dramatist is not
so much re-writing as re-voicing the text as he asks
us to listen again to some of the all-too-familiar sounds
of HAMLET and find them, in the context of the excited
commentary of the Director of the rehearsal and his
interactions with his actors, resonant with unexpected
meanings. Thus the Director prefaces the entrance
of the ghost of Hamlet's father with a characteristic
emphasis: "And every line has a political double
meaning" The quoted language of HAMLET, already
evocative of a Denmark in crisis, is coloured by
an even more insistently political vocabulary:
"revolution", "counter-coup" and "civil war". At the
heart of things is a conflicted young Hamlet who must
choose to be loyal to his father or to act as a free man.
To portray this crisis the important sounds are those
forms of speech which are most flagrantly equivocating

in the first place, forms which the Director is most
anxious to point up. So the exasperated Director in
Act Two protests at the way other interpreters cut out
all the riddles in the tragedy, "the riddles and puns that
add up to nothing less than the meaning of the entire
g'damn work of art". "Who's there?" will be answered,
then, in a surprising way in a play devoted to
unriddling this dramatic universe by dwelling on
truths hidden in the cryptic idioms of those conjoined
arch-equivocators, Hamlet and the Old Gravedigger.
The tragic Hamlet has often been seen to be a quibbling
clown, whether in Lacan's psychoanalytical approach
or David Tennant's recent virtuosic performance at
Stratford-upon-Avon. But it is here that this version
makes its most original move, exceeding say Harold
Bloom's observation in *How to Read and Why* (2000)
that "Only the gravedigger-clown is able to offer
Hamlet some companionship in wit" or James Shapiro's
contention in *1599* (2005) that Hamlet may clown in
much of the first half of the play but yields that function
to the gravedigger in the second. But here we are led to
discover, behind or beneath the common addiction to
word play of these apparently accidentally juxtaposed
characters, the Joker in the pack, the spirit of that
long-dead jester Yorick. As the Director insists:
"We want the audience to be absolutely astonished
when the ghost of Yorick fills up the stage."

Equivocation, then, blends with the way in which
this most haunted and haunting of tragedies is here
renewed by a doubling of its ghostliness. Freed gives
paradoxical presence—nay, agency—to the absent
Yorick. No modern re-writing of Hamlet has given such
prominence to this offstage personage, if we except the
Sternean trifle "Yorick" by Salman Rushdie (*East, West,*
1994), in which Hamlet revenges himself on his father
by exploiting the jester's jealousy. The accepted visual
representation of Yorick, which Freed retains, is the

iconic skull. To Jonathan Bate, for instance, in his
The Genius of Shakespeare (1997), this prop is contrasted
sharply as icon with the complex suggestiveness of
Hamlet's book, seeing it as "a straightforward figure",
a *memento mori*. But Freed goes beyond this and
conjures up both its manifest freight of nostalgia
for a carefree childhood and its unexpected power
to offer him an inspiriting vision of a future free of
subjection to reactionary authority. Bolder still, Freed
has Hamlet recognise Yorick's ghost in the very person
of the quibbling Clown, the Old Gravedigger as Freed
prefers to call him, beneath whose mask lurks that
supremely creative and liberating player with words,
Shakespeare. To bring this coup about Freed has shifted
Hamlet's centre of gravity to the graveyard, away from
the more usual focal scenes, whether it be the staging
and reception of THE MOUSETRAP or Hamlet's
confrontation of his mother in her bedroom. That is
the earthy and earthing place where wild Hamlet may
first appear to become a different person and the play
appears to swerve from the course that HAMLET had
been taking in the previous four acts. Here "the old
Revenge plot" is jettisoned (in truth, suspended) and
displaced by what Freed calls the "narrative", what
Frank Kermode in *The Genesis of Secrecy* would call the
"occult" sense, which is in this Director's perspective
the true end of Shakespeare's play. For the Director,
this means an exorcism of the Bad Ghost, "the false
king Hamlet". Disabling the engine of the revenge
play which has entrapped Hamlet for a time in
the machinations of the Court, he conjures up an
alternative father figure in "the true fool", the Good
Ghost. Now, in this final scene , young Hamlet is
shown as having changed, forsaken his regal role,
finally buried his father and through the witty
mediation of the Clown found his true identity,
as the Clown prince who is also the wise Fool. In

the original tragedy, Hamlet may, beyond this scene, reach a fatalistic calm before his achieved revenge and death, but here he is given an inspired festive sending-off with the joyful Prince and the Old Gravedigger singing together what the playwright calls "Yorick's Song", (that is, Hamlet's "Imperious Caesar..."). Then, what was anticipated when Hamlet vigorously embraced the Players on their riotous entrance in Act One and established his fellowship with them, he joins the company in a jig, the kind of dance which customarily concluded Elizabethan plays and which Freed here adapts beautifully to his novel context. The neo-Nietzschean death-defying effect is similar to that so stirringly achieved by the chorus of "The bells of hell go ding a-ling a-ling for you and not for me" which ends Brendan Behan's THE HOSTAGE (1958).

This induction of Hamlet into a quasi-familial bonding and solidarity with the group supports an interpretation of Freed's political mission in the play which has affinities with that of his contemporary, the outstanding English radical playwright Edward Bond. Bond wrote in 1995: "Hamlet discovers his soul. I want the character to discover society". Both dramatists seek, though often by different means, to save the great protagonist from a reading of HAMLET that views him in isolation from the socio-political dimension. In Freed's case this is wholly consistent with his central dramatic concerns. Play after play is devoted to the business of saving, a theme announced most blatantly in his one-act *tour de force*, HOW SHALL WE BE SAVED? In his broadly contemporary plays one might interpret this concern as "How shall we save America (from itself)?" Even in his moving study of James Joyce's almost-last days in IS HE STILL DEAD?, there is the implicit desire, as in this HAMLET, to save the creative spirit, not from death, but from deathliness, to inspire a last-ditch hope in the teeth of a generally experienced social constriction.

Like many serious dramatists Freed is fiercely gripped by the imagination of alternatives, to borrow the Jamesian phrase. For example, in this play he underlines the contrast already apparent in HAMLET between a familial ideal (nostalgia for a dead father, a bantering bond between brother and sister) and the grim actualities of the dysfunctional family by emphasising the latter through conspicuously stylised choreography, tableaux and sound-effects. The horrifying scene where the supremely patriarchal Polonius infantilises his grown-up offspring is a piece of pure expressionism, comparable to the sinister dream-like stage pictures often contrived by Edward Bond. By contrast, he invents a genial father-son relation between the two Clowns, as Old and Young Gravediggers, which he can claim is "the only healthy relationship in the entire play". Crucially, his double-sided Hamlet can in the space of the rehearsed play be free to choose another family: as character, to affiliate himself to a non-authoritarian father; as actor, to participate in an harmonious theatrical ensemble, the most plausible exemplification of the "tribe" or counterculture which challenges the conspiratorial world of the power-brokers or what in THE DEVIL'S ADVOCATE Freed has a character call "the terrible players".

Re-writing the "myth" of HAMLET, the revenge tragedy, Freed gives the protagonist his ghost of a chance—to live, fully and lovingly, not to die in an immoral cause. In the playwright's long-standing passion for re-writing both cultural myths and literary classics (one thinks of his fictional meditations on Nixon post-Watergate in SECRET HONOR, about Eichmann on trial in THE WHITE CROW and Bush

out-of-office in PATIENT NO.1, of his FAUST IN
HEAVEN, the Oedipal drama in CHILD OF LUCK
or the Odyssean substratum to CIRCE AND BRAVO),
he is drawn to intensely dramatic endgames.
He chooses to put his characters under the apocalyptic
pressure of their last days in ways which recall the
tightening-screw forms of his beloved Greek tragedians
and such claustrophobic moderns as Ibsen and Beckett.
The endgame of this HAMLET is uncanny, a thing
unknown returns in a different form, and is played out
in the confines of the graveyard, even in and about the
grave itself. In these endgames, Freed's characters often
succumb to a kind of madness, hysteria or (sometimes
justified) paranoia. Hamlet's "antic disposition" already
possesses the kind of ambiguity which Freed delights
to exploit, a serio-comic state which may aesthetically
evade the straitjacket of a superficial naturalistic
characterisation and politically combat the limiting
categorisations and cold rationalisations which govern
the oppressive state with the force of a Dionysiac
passion and unpredictable humour.

What may strike us as authentically alternative about
Freed's re-visioning of the iconic Hamlet? It is partly a
matter of intensification and purposeful simplification.
So the prison-like Court is a nightmarish vision, the
objective correlative of the kind of censoring and
persecuting civil power which has sought to crush
critical spirits like Freed in the U S A, but the reach
of this vision is wider. Freed sees his own resistance,
his "speaking truth to power", in the context of a long
and noble history of playwrights "great and potentially
great", from Aristophanes to Dario Fo, who have
attracted the attention of the censors or the secret
police by their taboo-breakings and refusals to conform.
No direct references are made to specifically American
abuses, but the Director in speech and manner is
plainly an American contemporary and the image

he strives to project is informed by Freed's own
unfortunate political and cultural experiences, while
those who operate the system of surveillance and brutal
control, like Polonius, Claudius and his sycophantic
minions (a bevy of spies peep out from holes around
the set), and even Hamlet's father from beyond the
grave, are considerably less shaded than in the original,
not just formidably tyrannical or deceitful but farcically
grotesque (Polonius and Claudius engage in an
undignified scramble for possession of Hamlet's letter,
a menaced Claudius clutches his testicles). Even
Horatio, who was always "the straight man" to Hamlet,
is represented as enslaved by "the Revenge Plot
conveyer belt", not in on the "narrative", and much less
of a bosom-pal to Hamlet than the Old Gravedigger.
In CIRCE AND BRAVO Freed had used an extract from
Horatio's penultimate speech, "And let me speak to the
yet unknowing world/How these things came about"
as one of the epigraphs, but the irony of the subsequent
too-external catalogue of disasters in that celebrated
summing-up is clarified by the way this Horatio,
significantly asleep in the climactic recognition scene
at the end , is constitutionally unable to elucidate those
"things standing thus unknown" of which Hamlet has
spoken. Such changes help to focus attention more than
ever on a bright, witty, hyper-sensitive, bewildered
but wildly energetic young protagonist—a redeemable
Hamlet, one who is capable of being transformed.

The most innovative aspect of the play is, of course,
its form, boldly announced in its title. Not only does
the play promise some sort of fresh perspective on
Shakespeare's tragedy, it frames that within a supposed
modern day rehearsal, combining thus allusions to two
distinctive dramatic genres. The latter may be slightly
less well known, although the play which shows us a
rehearsal in progress is as old as Shakespeare himself.
The antics of the rude mechanicals in A MIDSUMMER

NIGHT'S DREAM spring to mind, whilst HAMLET itself with its pivotal play-within-a-play gives us a Hamlet who, as gifted amateur actor and connoisseur of the theatre, is himself in his advice to the players visiting Elsinore on the verge of assuming the role of a director about to rehearse his troupe. Plays devoted to representing a rehearsal at length and exploiting it for satirical purposes are exemplified in the English-language tradition by the burlesques of Buckingham's THE REHEARSAL (1672) and Sheridan's THE CRITIC (1779), where the monstrous claims to authority of writer-directors made, respectively, by Bayes and Puff are farcically exposed. Their image derives in some respects from the bustling self-importance of Bottom. "HAMLET" IN REHEARSAL, has more in common with modern tragicomedies revolving around the play-within-the-play. There are such Continental precursors as Pirandello's SIX CHARACTERS IN SEARCH OF AN AUTHOR (1921) and Anouilh's LA RÉPÉTITION (1950), which, though in part satirical, tend to exploit rehearsal practices for to play a metatheatrical game, exploring the ambiguous relations of art to life, and make a bitterly disillusioned comment on humanity. In modern Anglophone theatre, the outstanding overtly politicised images of rehearsal are Edward Bond's THE SEA (1973) and Samuel Beckett's anomalous CATASTROPHE (1982). The hyper-energetic detective-Director of HAMLET in Freed's play is neither the sacred monster or petty tyrant of Bond, nor an obtuse Pirandellian *Direttore-capocomico*, nor Beckett's the totalitarian sadist. He is more of a Prospero-like benign dictator, a sophisticated theatre-practitioner whose rehearsal appears to be as detailed and prescriptive as Shaw rashly assumed Shakespeare's to be, that is, Shavian. Yet, in spite of his tenacious commitment to a novel and deliberated vision of the text, which echoes Freed's own

straightforward exposition of the "Yorick axis"
in HAMLET (given as part of a Master Class at the
Old Vic in London in 2007), he can be taken by surprise,
as when in Act Two he suddenly makes a connection
between Hamlet's identification of the Old Clown as
the Ghost of Yorick and Hamlet's earlier seemingly
incongruous address of his father's ghost as "old mole",
or admits that he cannot immediately resolve an
important issue raised by the actor playing the Queen
as to whether she sees the Ghost: "Let's sleep on it."
And he can allow creative input from members of his
cast at such turning points in the rehearsal as when,
first, the actress playing Gertrude, then, the actor
playing Hamlet are in danger of "stopping the play" as
they challenge the Director, realising—in keeping with
one of Freed's major strategies—the alternative paths
the story might take if their characters should choose
differently. This is consistent with Freed's concern
both with dramatising ambivalence, especially in
his depiction of Hamlet struggling to free himself
of imposed or inherited burdens, and with breaking
the theatrical illusion in order to excite the audience's
thoughtful participation in a dynamic re-assessment
of the classic.

Another response to "Who's there?" is, after all,
the actors. Sometimes the Director makes the point
by suddenly taking part himself, as does the Stage
Manager in Thornton Wilder's OUR TOWN (1938),
an earlier classic American study in laying bare the
device or showing the works. Up to a point this is not
so very unusual in a rehearsal with absentees, or where
a cast is uneconomically large, or where there is a
need to show an actor how to do it, but here that is
not the case. For instance, when he climbs into the
grave, seemingly anticipating profane intrusions by
Hamlet and Laertes in the scene which should normally
succeed Freed's finale, it is to demonstrate forcefully

what lies at the heart of the drama, "where the
bodies are buried". It is one with the *earthiness* of
his interpretation, shared with Margareta Grazia's
"HAMLET" WITHOUT HAMLET (2008), one of
the most interesting among recent studies of the play.
It permeates his persistent physicalisations: seen at its
simplest in having Hamlet and Ophelia embrace, but
more extravagantly in the extreme reactions, mimings
and jiggings now assigned to the characters. Much extra
weight is given to certain props, like Hamlet's " painted
sword" or the Gravedigger's stoup of liquor. The actors
are instructed to act out more graphically their recoils
from the stench of the graveyard, and Guildenstern,
more puzzlingly, is told to blow his nose. Although
the Director steps into the roles of figures of power like
Claudius, the Ghost of Old Hamlet and the First Player,
his impassioned anti-authoritarian designs usually
stand out in relief. and are tinged with some reassuring
touches of comedy, as when he catches himself quoting
the wrong play in the opening scene or, on finding that
the property rat does not work, commands: "Cut the
rat" On the other hand, his urge to unite his company
in a rival family to the dysfunctional ones on display in
Denmark, although it may risk the taint of the "luvvie",
is crucial to the play's implicit defence of theatre
as ideally exemplifying, in its eagerly collaborative
endeavours, the good society . Judged as a naturalistic
representation of a director at rehearsal, he may come
across as overexcited by his "code-cracking" mission
(for re-interpreters of classic plays are often out to
uncover the secrets of the text invisible to earlier
spectators). He may, like Wilder's garrulous Stage
Manager, seem rather prolix in his instructor role
(especially in Act Two), whilst as tender patriarch
in this improvised stage family it may be that he does
not have to cope with enough of the organic tensions
and contentions which would naturally arise in the

rehearsal room community . And there are all kinds of
rehearsal. His is a curious partial rehearsal. It begins
plausibly enough with house lights up, tea-making and
warm-ups *et al.* It covers only certain carefully selected
moments in the script and works with actors who
are virtually word-perfect, with most of their moves
already blocked, but with the technical effects still
being "roughed out", while the whole is half-dressed.
In the rehearsal, we might expect interruptions and
improvisations, but lengthy interjections and directions
to skip parts that don't further the "argument", as the
Director sees it, give it a special driven atmosphere.
In the hands of an increasingly more eloquent and
resourceful Director we may come to realise that he is
deploying the same theatre-poetic skills as the author,
his enthusiastic suggestions matched by many nuanced
stage directions in print. This rehearsal play/play
rehearsal grows steadily into something gradually
more removed from representation of any customary
practices and impresses as an impassioned excursion
into an alternative reality in a manner familiar to those
who have encountered Freed's daring lyrical leaps
and rhetorical heightening in plays like CIRCE AND
BRAVO and THE DEVIL'S ADVOCATE, but one
which, while reflecting the author's own fantasies,
keeps in touch with his real-life experience of
numerous creative partnerships with actors and
writers. By the exquisite close of the play there may
be a gently insinuated, rueful humour in the Director's
acknowledgement of the Quixotism of his effort to
disrupt the customary sorry saga of revenge, to derail
that notorious plot, by his detective-like pursuit
and exposition of its hidden truths. He must accept
that not only will the familiar HAMLET be staged ,
conventionally enough, again and again in theatres
across the globe but he will himself have to rehearse
it in full the very next day. As Freed has himself

pragmatically recognised in his extra-dramatic writing,
any *catharsis*, or purging of false consciousness, such as
he hopes to have achieved here in saving Hamlet from
having to play "the Prince" as the avenging tool of the
repressive regime, may be transitory, yes, but must be
constantly renewed. Raymond Chandler once wrote
that "The detective story is a tragedy with a happy
ending". The Director of this strange detective story
clings to something like that humane faith, when he
invites us to join in the song and dance, to live in the
moment of hopefulness, as if at a wake rather than a
funeral.

"Who's there?", I ask for one more time. Many readers
and spectators, I trust. It is very pleasing that this
play-text is now to become available to a wider public
than that first very appreciative audience in York
and that from this publication we may expect many
subsequent performances of a fine addition to the
distinguished body of work by one of America's
foremost dramatists. The play should have an appeal
to the many readers and spectators already familiar
with the Elizabethan classic, who will find the work
beguilingly defamiliarised, as well as to those who
may respond to the powerful moral and political
vision of a consistent American radical and a tirelessly
inventive man of the theatre.

Alistair Stead, Leeds, September 2008

MISE-EN-SCENE

The "in rehearsal" of this production is a concept aimed
at deepening the interpretation and the experience of
Shakespeare's masterpiece. The concept is not meant
as a conceit or a device nor yet another bright idea
or substitute for, arguably, the greatest single work of
art in the history of civilization. This Rehearsal/Run-
through is simply a record of a search—as are all
serious rehearsals—for a way out of the prison of
the Plot that is Denmark; and a comprehension of
the ghosts and bad dreams that haunt the Prince's
all too human heart and tragic imagination.

The intention in this reconstruction of the timeless work
is to reveal the congruence of the politics *in* the play
and the politics *of* the play and thus, at one stroke, to
pierce their double censorship.

An interval is indicated between Acts Two and Three of
Shakespeare's HAMLET.

THE CAST

Multiple role playing by each actor, except for HAMLET,
*is in the spirit of the Rehearsal approach to the old revenge
saga that Shakespeare inherited. This plan is flexible.
One is suggested below.*

ACTOR: 1: BERNARDO; YOUNG GRAVEDIGGER; LAERTES;
GUILDENSTERN; ACTOR

ACTOR: 2: FRANCISCO; REYNALDO; ROSENCRANTZ;
ACTOR; ASSISTANT STAGE MANAGER

ACTOR: 3: THE DIRECTOR; KING CLAUDIUS; GHOST; THE
OLD ACTOR *or* FIRST PLAYER

ACTOR: 4: THE STAGE MANAGER; QUEEN GERTRUDE;
OPHELIA

ACTOR: 5: POLONIUS; OLD GRAVEDIGGER

ACTOR: 6: HORATIO; ACTOR; COURTIER

ACTOR: 7: HAMLET

THE STAGE

The entire stage is black: floor; platforms and steps; curtains; masking flats and returns.

The Director's/Stage Management table is down stage, out of the action. Also in the down stage areas are the tea table and chairs for actors to use when they are not rehearsing or waiting to enter.

There is no furniture as such, only rectangular black "elements". These elements, singly or together, are used for seats, thrones, beds, graves, etc...

There should be at least three platforms of differing size and height.

Swords and daggers should be wooden staves or old rehearsal instruments. All props should be improvised or incomplete.

Costumes range from street clothes to rehearsal skirts for the women. There can be a scattering of "period" coats, hats, cloaks, etc. from the Wardrobe Department.

The technical booth or space should be open during the rehearsal; sound and light adjustments take place "live" during the run-through.

This HAMLET project is dedicated to the inspiring and inspired Artistic Director of York Theatre Royal, Damian Cruden. And to the entire Company at Y T R, beginning with Carol Morrill, who made my Playwright-in-Residency in their great theater such an adventure and joy.

And to Nick Rusling, Edward Pearce, and Alistair Stead, scholars and friends, for their rare generosity and enthusiasm.

PROLOGUE

(House lights are up. Stage empty; technician on a ladder, adjusting a lamp. Work-light on stage produces deep shadows. Somewhere a radio is broadcasting news on the hour, then an old Dixieland instrumental.)

*(*STAGE MANAGER *enters and begins to make tea. Actors drift in from the wings and down the aisles, through the auditorium.)*

*(*DIRECTOR *enters, confers with* STAGE MANAGER, *greets actors, fixes cup of tea.... After an interval,* DIRECTOR *blows his whistle and assembles the company to begin their physical and vocal warm-ups.)*

DIRECTOR: ...stretch, stretch—five, six, seven, eight... Head and neck... And shoulders up, high, and down slowly, and leave your chest high, and again; chest stationary, and again... And, bend from the waist, knees loose, and five, six, seven, eight, and again...

*(*DIRECTOR *moves among the company to find and eliminate tensions in the actors.)*

DIRECTOR: ...Alright. Breathe. Yawn: and Ha— Ya, Ya, Ya...suppressed yawn— Ya— Ya—jaw down and forward. Ya— Ya— Ya *(Loud yawns).*

*(*DIRECTOR *and company move through the voice and diction drills.)*

DIRECTOR: The tongue, the teeth, the lips—the tongue, the teeth, the lips—tongue low and relaxed, and vibrate the tongue and lips ... good.

...Drum— Bel— Tin— Nine— Gong:

Don't strain, Drummmm—and pull from the belt—
pull, pull, and one final pull from the diaphragm,
and release, and push *out*, and, again... And

"A drum, a drum, Macbeth doth commmm—"
(Laughter) Sorry, wrong play— Now, Belllll,
"And shallll I couplllle Hellll?"...

Now, nine—nine—nine—nine— "It is I, Hamlet the
Dannnne?"

Don't strain— "Bloody, Bawdy Villain / treacherous,
lecherous, kinnndless villainnn— O,Vengeannnnce!"
..."V" and "Z": "Seemmzzz, madam, nay it 'tizz, I know
not seemmmzzz." And, "I did lovvvve you once." And,
"The madness wherein now he ravvvzzzz"; again...

And pull from the diaphragm—and release—and
push *out*, that's it.

(The DIRECTOR *monitors each actor's production. Hands on,
smoothing tensions away. A mobile phone sounds. All
freeze—until the culprit dashes to silence the villain.)*

DIRECTOR: ...Consonants: F, T, P, K, D—quicker,
slower— "speak the speech I *pray* you...*t*rippingly
on the *t*ongue", and, "the *t*ime i*z* ou*t* o*v* join*t* , O curse*d*
spi*t*e tha*t* ever I wa*z* born to se*t* i*t* righ*t*." ... "Now could
I drin*k* ho*t* bloo*d*." Again. Again. Drin*K* ho*T* bloo*D*!
One hundred percent today, my friends, every word
and every syllable of every word. Thank you!

(They all applaud each other.)

DIRECTOR: Good. Relax...the drill today is to stop and
start wherever we've had problems at turning points
and moments of truth. And tomorrow, of course, is a
tech/dress rehearsal. We'll have some lights and sound
today, but what's paramount is that you remember that
"Denmark is a prison". The world of this play—outside
and inside—is a prison. And every character in this
world—our world—has one aim and one aim only and

that is to "escape". But each of you can only escape
in your own way. *(Pointing)* Yours is drink; yours is
power, of course; Rosencrantz and Guildenstern, denial
and treachery; Ophelia, illusion, daydreams, madness;
Horatio, loyalty—I'm not talking words, I'm talking
"intention": *obsession, compulsion, starvation—prison—
madhouse—torture chamber—actual prison...*

(DIRECTOR sits, and draws the company around him.)

DIRECTOR: *"Anagnorisis"*...

STAGE MANAGER: He's an old Greek.

(They all smile.)

DIRECTOR: The Truth of *this* production, of this *Hamlet*,
of this *rehearsal*—today, now: Hamlet wants to go back
to Wittenberg. Wittenberg is the future. He needs to go.
But Denmark forces him to stay. His Mother begs him,
his Uncle, the King, forbids it, and, then, the god-
damned Ghost comes clanking up in full armor from
Hell, itself, to chain him to Elsinore—to revenge, and to
history... So the Prince has no "future" except continual
murder and vengeance. His future in art and the life of
the mind at Wittenberg is foreclosed. He is sentenced to
life in prison here in this castle. And, so, in total despair
and nausea, he retreats into "madness". *(He rubs his
scalp.)* Then, comes the miracle of the play: in his
madness—feigned and real—the Prince re-discovers,
remembers a sensation, a taste from long ago,
from Yorick's lips, of *the only true escape*—the taste
of freedom. And that is "the Yorick Axis" of this
production. In other words, what we have here is a
new play! *(He toasts company with a cup of tea.)* Hamlet's
drive for freedom through his "antic disposition",
his playwriting and acting, his defection to the pirates,
his loyalty and love for Horatio and the soldiers, his
worship of the actors and their art and, above all, his
final reverence for the Old Gravedigger, before whom,

at last, the prince lays down his arms. That's the key,
the key scene, the clock that strikes thirteen, in the
graveyard, casting doubt on everything that's gone
before...so hang onto your intentions, today, like a
lifeline, a burning thread, for you to follow out of
the power politics and the hell-hole of your Prison....
There's one way out. One way out of all prisons. You
can dig your way out. The Old Gravedigger and his
Apprentice—in this production, his *son*—they know the
way. But no-one else in the play, in the prison, has the
courage to follow these so-called "Clowns" down into
that labyrinth of freedom; no-one, that is, except the
Prince, himself. *(He puts his arm around the actor playing*
HAMLET.*)* His body's his prison. "Hamlet" and the
"Prince of Denmark" are locked up in the same body.
Doubleness. Claustrophobia... The others, all and each
in their own way, commit suicide as their way out.
Only Hamlet and his "people" —descended from
Yorick, the god disguised as the King's Jester—
only Yorick's tribe, the Soldiers, the Actors, the Pirates,
the Gravediggers: Hamlet's people, Yorick's tribe—
they, and only they, have the taste of freedom in their
mouths, and know, at least dimly, for what it is they
hunger.... Thank you, and as Bob Altman used to say,
"Have fun!" —and he meant it seriously.

*(*DIRECTOR *and company mingle, touch, relate: a kind*
of family.)

DIRECTOR: ...Alright, so have fun. We'll go straight
through the problems and the turning points, and
even the "Moments of Truth" *(Laughter)*, as far as we
can—there may be a few cuts.

SSTAGE MANAGER: Can we cut the rat?

(General hilarity)

DIRECTOR: Very funny, very funny—you make me believe that "Denmark is a prison" —and I'll consider cutting the rat.

(Company reaction)

DIRECTOR: Alright? Let's go.

STAGE MANAGER: Places, please. First Act beginners.

(The company leaves the stage for their places. The DIRECTOR speaks to the light/sound booth.)

DIRECTOR: ...Ladies and gentlemen, do your best, technically, just rough it in. We won't stop, use work lights if you have to. (To STAGE MANAGER) I'll be right back, take the house lights out and start the Chant on a one minute count.

(DIRECTOR exits. STAGE MANAGER cues the Gregorian Chants tape, and fades the house lights.)

(Complete dark and the Chants for another sixty seconds. Then, a sliver of cold light from the frozen moon.)

(From out of the blackness comes DIRECTOR's voice:)

DIRECTOR: *(From darkness)* ...Gentlemen—you have the pitch darkness...you have the cold... Tech. Booth, take the moon out, please— You have the politics, the State of Emergency, now in its sixth week! ...You have your long entrance through this wind chill... You can hear, but you can't see the others.... Who is it, who's there? The Ghost? One of the King's spies, or assassins? Or a spy or agent of Fortinbras? ...Norway smells Denmark's weakness. Fortinbras is on the march. Revenge is on the march! So—come towards each other—actually ready to fight, to kill, or be killed... It's freezing but you're sweating—use your noses and your ears to find your way through this darkness.... O K—go. Cue the church bells, and sneak the moonlight on a twenty count.

(Bells toll midnight. Chant fades. Silence. Footsteps)

(Shakespeare's Act One, Scene One)

(One soldier enters from up stage, the other soldier from the back of the auditorium and comes down the aisle. The moonbeam casts a huge ghost-like shadow.)

BERNARDO: Who's there?

FRANCISCO: Nay, answer me. Stand and unfold yourself.

BERNARDO: Long live the King!

FRANCISCO: Bernardo.

BERNARDO: He.

FRANCISCO: You come most carefully upon your hour.

BERNARDO: 'tis now struck twelve—

DIRECTOR: *(Blows whistle)* Good. "Nay, answer me!" Just take it again from "Long live the King". We have to grasp that this "Long live the King" is meant for the ears of the King's spies—out there in the dark. Tonight could be the night. The King could massacre the Prince, Hamlet, and all his loyalists, starting with you—or, Horatio and Hamlet could be on their way to give the word to go to ground, or to start the uprising— anything is possible—*anything!* —that's why everybody is seeing ghosts—including the audience if you two fight to maintain control over your bowels and your vowels—they'll believe in ghosts if you believe in them—and when the Ghost, of the murdered King, gives the word, *then!* —then the uprising begins! —with Hamlet leading the troops—and you two right behind him! That's their fantasy and that's the story of the first scene... Take it from the top, please. And Gentlemen, you have to create the night, the terror, the blackness of darkness: close your eyes—go!

BERNARDO: *(Low)* Who's there?

FRANCISCO: *(Low)* Nay, answer me. Stand and unfold yourself.

BERNARDO: *(Loud)* Long live the King!

DIRECTOR: Now, open your eyes.

FRANCISCO: *(Natural tone)* Bernardo.

BERNARDO: He.

FRANCISCO: You come most carefully upon your hour.

BERNARDO: 'tis now struck twelve... Get thee to bed, Francisco.

FRANCISCO: ...'tis bitter cold, and I am sick at heart.

DIRECTOR: Good. Better. Exactly: "Bitter cold", "sick at heart": no Ghost, no sign, no signal—another midnight come and gone... Alright, let's go on: Horatio comes in, the Ghost does appear; Horatio is convinced and they decide to tell Hamlet *today*! O K, Scene Two, please. Cue the "flourish". Let's try the red and green lights.

(Shakespeare's Act One, Scene Two)

(Royal music for KING, QUEEN *and court as they enter.* KING *is played by* DIRECTOR.)

*(*KING *and* POLONIUS *stand on the center platform. Between them a jester crouches holding the crown on a velvet pillow. But which of the two older men, on either side of the crown, is the King?)*

*(*QUEEN *stands alone some distance from the royal platform. Next,* HAMLET *enters and stops at his mother's side. She secretly grasps her son's hand for a moment. The royal courtiers are played by all the other cast members.)*

(The ensemble moves constantly in a choreography of gossip and treason, a hissing echo of KING's *first speech [The Power Party Line]).*

(This echolalia is sadistically enunciated and orchestrated by the chorus:)

CHORUS: *(The court)* "...Though yet of Hamlet our dear brother's death the memory be green..."

(The red and green lights play over the moving clump of bodies as over a monster of the deep.)

(One of the two older men on the platform tries to speak, but to no avail. The gestalt of gossiping thugs never leave any space for KING.*)*

KING: ...Though, ah...though yet of, ah...

(Finally, the other older man, POLONIUS, *clears his throat. At the sound of the power, of the old regime, the court freezes.)*

(Claudius, the KING, *steps off his platform as if into a troubled sea and walks a dangerous circuit among the living dead of the Court.)*

POLONIUS: Hm—mmm... *(Silence)*

KING: *(Coming down)* ...Though yet of Hamlet our dear brother's death the memory be green, and that it us befitted to bear our hearts in grief—

*(*DIRECTOR *steps out of* KING's *character to address the company.*

DIRECTOR: Look—don't make it easy for the King. Make him break you. This is Denmark—kill or be killed. Today is the day—six weeks in—Claudius consolidates his power, or they overthrow him and eat him alive!

*(*DIRECTOR *resumes his role of* KING.*)*

KING: ...To bear our hearts in grief, and our whole Kingdom to be contracted in one brow of woe, yet so far hath discretion fought with nature that we with wisest sorrow think on him together with remembrance of ourselves.

(On the word "ourselves" KING *threatens the court. They begin to shrink.)*

KING: Therefore our sometimes sister, *now our queen,* th' imperial jointress to this *warlike* state...have we taken to wife...

(KING *has conquered. The courtiers, like apes, laugh and clap. All except* HAMLET.)

(KING *takes the crown and Gertrude's arm and leads his prize up on to the platform. This leaves* HAMLET *alone, in no man's land.)*

(*Silence.* KING's *eyes turn on* HAMLET—*so do all the courtiers'.)*

KING: ...But now, my cousin Hamlet and my son—

HAMLET: A little more than kin and less than kind.

KING: How is it that the clouds still hang on you?

HAMLET: Not so, my lord; I am too much in the sun.

QUEEN: Good Hamlet, cast thy nighted colour off...
Do not forever with thy vailed lids
Seek for thy noble father in the dust.
Thou know'st 'tis common; all that lives must die,
Passing through nature to eternity.

HAMLET: Ay, madam, it is common.

(*The* DIRECTOR *blows softly on his whistle and leaves his platform.*

DIRECTOR: Gertrude...take it again, remember—this is all about *real-politic:* "Wash your face—life is cheap, life is violent—have a drink, burn those black clothes— give your uncle a chance, he's as good a man as your father. Better! Younger—ha—ha" ...Look, she's half drunk, they all are—except Hamlet, and he's intoxicated with nausea. —So, again.

QUEEN: Good Hamlet, cast thy nighted colour off...

DIRECTOR: That's better. Think Bette Davis—think, ah, who? (*Laughter*)

ACTOR: (QUEEN) Helen Mirren?

DIRECTOR: Think, "I need a drink. I need a nap.
I, ah, need, you know, I *need*."

(QUEEN *repeats the speech with a kind of broken-hearted gaiety.*)

DIRECTOR: (*Blows whistle*) Yes—it's coming...cut to
the Court's exit, and go right into the soliloquy...
And everyone on the beat, a half line behind the
King—and do not spare the gloating!

(*The court exits echoing* KING.)

KING & COURT:
Why, 'tis a loving and a fair reply,
Be as ourself in Denmark—Madam, come.
This gentle and unforced accord of Hamlet
Sits smiling to my heart, in grace whereof
No jocund health that Denmark drinks today
But the great canon to the clouds shall tell,
And the King's rouse the heaven shall bruit it again,
Respeaking earthly thunder. Come away.

(*Flourish. All but* HAMLET *exit.*)

(HAMLET, *alone, studies/smells the silence.... He steps to
the edge of* KING's *platform, but does not mount.... He sits,
then, on the corner of the riser. Hangs his head with a
groaning/vomiting exhalation—then another and another
as he slowly lies back flat on his back.*)

(HAMLET *moans softly, then tenses and listens. He sees or
smells a rat, sits up, rises slowly, searching. He spies the
rat—* "Aggggh!" *—and bolts away in the opposite direction.*)

(HAMLET *leaps through a drapery to escape, only to flush
out a court operative hidden there. The spy screams too,
and scuttles away.*)

(*However, at this rehearsal the "rat" prop does not function.*)

DIRECTOR: Goddammit, where's the g'damn rat!?

STAGE MANAGER: Where's the rat?

ACTOR: *(Off stage)* The string broke.

(Silence)

DIRECTOR: ...Cut the rat.

(Silence)

HAMLET: *(Actor)* ...So—what about the spy?

DIRECTOR: *(Pause)* Try the, ah, moral equivalent of the rat. *(Pause)* The spy. Smell *him.*

HAMLET: *(Actor)* You mean—

DIRECTOR: Smell him. See what happens. What would Hamlet do!? —Let's go.

(Again, HAMLET *groans and lies flat. Again, he tenses and listens. This time he rises with a prehensile stealth. Controls his breathing and his limbs—stalks his prey: shocks the spy with a shouting leap into the drapes.)*

(The spy tears away. HAMLET *vents his outrage and plunges into his soliloquy.)*

(In the dark,a soft, intense)

DIRECTOR: *Yeah!*

HAMLET: —Ahhhhh! —Hah!
That this too too sullied flesh would melt
Thaw, and resolve itself into a dew,
Or that the Everlasting had not fixed
His canon 'gainst self slaughter! O God, God,
How weary, stale, flat and unprofitable
Seem to me all the uses of this world!
(He, almost unconsciously, begins a savage parody of KING *and* QUEEN; *followed by a series of mood swings. He stops twice to guard against any spy or eavesdropper.)*
...Frailty, thy name is woman!
A little month, or ere those shoes were old
With which she followed my poor father's body,

Like Niobe, all tears—why she, even she—
O, God, a beast that wants discourse of reason,
Would have mourned longer! —married with
my uncle, *(Pause)*
My father's brother, but no more like my father
Than I to Hercules. Within a month—she married.
(He is down again, on the platform, rolling in rage.
In rage, and something else, something sensual....)
O, most wicked speed, to post
With such dexterity to incestuous sheets!
(He, now, does hear someone. He recovers and contains
himself, tries to make his exit.)
It is not nor it cannot come to good.
But break, my heart, for I must hold my tongue.

(Enter HORATIO *and* BERNARDO.*)*

HORATIO: Hail to your lordship.

HAMLET: I am glad to see you well. *(Stops)* Horatio!
Or I do forget myself!

*(*HAMLET *and* HORATIO *embrace. The prince shakes and*
sobs for an instant. DIRECTOR *blows his whistle.)*

DIRECTOR: Alright—they confirm the ghost to him.
Hamlet doesn't want to believe it because then he'd
have to organise the counter-coup, *right now*—
so he takes the piss out of his

loyal pals, the soldiers—

HAMLET: Armed, say you?

ALL: *(Overlapping)* Armed, my lord.

HAMLET: From top to toe?

ALL: My lord, from head to foot.

HAMLET: *(Laughing)* Then saw you not his face!

DIRECTOR: *(From the dark)* Gotcha! Good—he can't believe it—but he does! O K—it works—go to the end, then right on to Scene Three.

(All but HAMLET *exit.)*

HAMLET: *(Hides in curtain)* My father's spirit—in arms! All is not well. I doubt some foul play. Would the night were come! Till then, sit still, my soul. Foul deeds will rise, though all the earth o'oerwhelm them, to men's eyes.

*(*HAMLET *exits, looking for hidden agents;* POLONIUS, LAERTES, OPHELIA *enter.)*

(Shakespeare's Act One, Scene Three)

*(*POLONIUS *and his children enter, the father talking and his off-spring listening. He talks and walks them in a circle, finally bringing them into a pool of light and forcing them to their knees.)*

POLONIUS: ...Aboard, Laertes, aboard, for shame!
The wind sits in the shoulder of your sail,
And you are stayed for...my blessings with thee.
And these few precepts in thy memory keep...
This above all, to thine own self be true—

DIRECTOR: Wait! Try this: Polonius, keep circling—make them dizzy—repeat "To thine own self" twice. Get into the pool of light and force them down—*(To Tech. Booth)*. Bring the Gregorian Chants in under the repetition, then build over the dialogue so that we see Polonius' lips moving but we can't hear the poison he's spewing, but we make our point: everybody—everybody from Attila the Hun to Adolph Hitler to George W Bush is to his "own self true". —O K. From the top, please.

*(*POLONIUS, LAERTES *and* OPHELIA *begin again. They circle.* DIRECTOR *follows; gestures for the Gregorian Chants, signals for the spotlight: orchestrates sound, light and actors.)*

*(POLONIUS talks, the children sink to their knees. The
DIRECTOR signals the chants, then a light change to create
a silhouette of the family tableau.)*

*(The children are prostrate. POLONIUS rants, unheard,
as the chants fill the world.)*

*(The icy wind of Scene Four rises and merges with the chants
as HAMLET enters the open ramparts.)*

(Shakespeare's Act One, Scene Four)

*(Enter HAMLET, HORATIO and BERNARDO. Chants down,
wind up and sounds of crashing waves.)*

HAMLET: The air bites shrewdly; it is very cold.

HORATIO: It is a nipping and an eager air.

HAMLET: What hour now?

*(They move with apprehension through the darkness,
the freezing wind, the roaring sea.)*

(From his table in the dark theater, DIRECTOR calls out:)

DIRECTOR: Not so fast. It's freezing. They're swimming
through a nightmare, a sea of ice and terror. Tonight's
the night: if they see the sign the revolution begins!
—So look for the sign of the Ghost, but pray that you
don't see it. *(To STAGE MANAGER)* More wind, and
moonlight— And every line has a political double
meaning.

HAMLET: ...What hour now?

HORATIO: I think it lacks of twelve.

BERNARDO: No, it is struck.

(Enter GHOST.)

HORATIO: Look, my lord, it comes.

*(They draw their rehearsal "swords", then turn them to
use as protective crucifixes. The DIRECTOR appears in the*

"Ghost's-Special". That cold moonlight beam spills over onto
HAMLET.*)*

HAMLET: Angels and ministers of—

DIRECTOR: *(Out of character)* Hold it. I'm sorry but it's
not good enough. The swords into crucifixes was very
clever, once upon a time, but the—

ACTOR: (HORATIO) The problem—

DIRECTOR: —The problem is it's a Catholic ghost in—

ACTOR: (HAMLET) —In a Lutheran country.

DIRECTOR: *(Pause)* That's not the problem.

ACTOR: *(Pause)* What is the problem?

DIRECTOR: To shriek or not to shriek. Garrick shrieked,
according to Doctor Johnson, and scared the bejesus out
of the *Ghost.* But that was *then. (Silence)* I don't know...
(Silence)

ACTOR: (HAMLET) ...Can we try just the light.

DIRECTOR: Without the Ghost? *(Pause)* Try it. What
would the Prince do?

HAMLET: I don't know.

DIRECTOR: What would he *want* to do?

HAMLET: Run away?

DIRECTOR: Bingo!

HAMLET: So—

DIRECTOR: So—Hamlet runs away—but the "Prince of
Denmark", he can't run away, he has to run *toward* the
"Royal Dane"!

(Pause)

HAMLET: ...What hour now?

HORATIO: I think it lacks of twelve.

BERNARDO: No, it is struck.

(Ghost light only, up)

HORATIO: *(A whisper)* Look, my lord, it comes...

*(*HORATIO *and* BERNARDO *are frozen.* HAMLET, *also,
until he finally takes baby steps toward the horror.)*

HAMLET: Angels and ministers of grace, defend us!...
Be thou a spirit of health or goblin damned...

DIRECTOR: Right. "Doubleness". Hamlet forces himself
to become the Prince of Denmark. To be loyal to the
Father/King against his whore Mother and the whole
world! To be his father's true son and *faithful* wife!
...And cut to, "Say, why is this...?"

HAMLET: Say, why is this? Wherefore? What should
we do?

HORATIO: It beckons you to go away with it—

BERNARDO: But do not go—

HORATIO: No, by no means.

HAMLET: It waves me still. —Go on, I'll follow thee.

HORATIO: Be ruled. You shall not go.

HAMLET: My fate cries out
And makes each petty arture in this body
As hardy as the Nemean lion's nerve.
Still am I called. Unhand me, gentlemen.
By heaven, I'll make a ghost of him that lets me!
I say, away! —Go on. I'll follow thee.

*(*GHOST *and* HAMLET *exit.* HORATIO *and* BERNARDO *talk
of following but they are rooted in terror to the spot.)*

(All dark, again; wind and waves sound overall.)

HORATIO: ...He waxes desperate with imagination.

BERNARDO: Let's follow. *(Pause)* 'Tis not fit thus to obey him.

HORATIO: Have after. *(Pause)* To what issue will this come?

BERNARDO: *(A whisper)* Something is rotten in the state of Denmark.

HORATIO: *(A whisper)* Heaven will direct it.

BERNARDO: Nay. *(Pause)* let's follow him.

(The DIRECTOR *returns.)*

DIRECTOR: Good. Bernardo's smelling his own terror as much as he is the rottenness of Denmark. —So, go to black, before they move, so we don't know whether or not they have the guts to follow Hamlet Senior and Junior on the long march to civil war, let alone a bloodbath with Fortinbras and his *berserkers. (To* HAMLET) Good. Now, the Prince is going to try to kill his other self—Hamlet—his "youth", his "observation", his genius, his memory—and live and die for the Ghost, alone. For revenge and only *revenge*! But, somehow, and this is Shakespeare's genius, Hamlet escapes the King and the Prince by putting on an "antic disposition" —that he doesn't know or remember is actually the Ghost of Yorick. So, it's Hamlet against the Prince, and the Ghost of Yorick against the Ghost of the King: *a fight to the finish!* ...O K— "*Adieu, adieu, adieu.* Remember me."

*(*GHOST-*light down and out. Dawn light slowly rising)*

HAMLET: *(He writes in a book.)* Ay, thou poor ghost, whiles memory holds a seat in this distracted "globe". Remember thee? Yea, from the table of my memory I'll wipe away all trivial, fond records, all saws of books, all forms, all pressures past, that youth and observation copied there,
(He writes.)
And thy commandment all alone shall live within the

book and volume of my brain, unmixed with baser
matter. Yes, by heaven!
(He writes.)
O most pernicious woman! O villain, villain, smiling
damned villain!
That one may smile and smile and be a villain. At least
I'm sure it may be so in Denmark.
(He writes.)
So, Uncle, there you are. Now to my word. It is *"adieu,
adieu,* remember me". I have sworn it.

VOICES: *(Off)* My lord—Lord Hamlet.

(HAMLET *almost jumps out of his skin as his friends run on.
He overwhelms them with melodrama one moment and the
wild comedic exchange with* GHOST *the next.)*

(Does HAMLET *throw his voice like a ventriloquist, to place
the "Ghost" under the stones? Truly, he is split in two,
caught between the King and the jester.)*

(HORATIO *and* BERNARDO, *off, looking for* HAMLET.*)*

HORATIO: My lord, my lord!

BERNARDO: Lord Hamlet!.

HORATIO: *(Off)* Heaven secure him!

HAMLET: *(To himself)* So be it.

BERNARDO: *(Off)* Illo, ho, ho, my lord!

HAMLET: Hillo, ho, ho, boy? Come, bird, come!

(DIRECTOR calls out from the dark.)

DIRECTOR: Again: "Hillo-ho" is the "Antic Disposition",
the Ghost of Yorick, *re-membering* Hamlet. The good
ghost, go with the good ghost—until the bad ghost
tears you away—tremendous pace, now. Go!

HAMLET: Hillo, ho, ho, boy! Come, bird, come!

BERNARDO: *(Entering)* How is't, my noble lord?

HORATIO: *(Entering)* What news, my lord?

HAMLET: O, wonderful!

HORATIO: Good my lord, tell it.

HAMLET: No, you will reveal it.

HORATIO: Not I, my lord, by heaven.

BERNARDO: Nor I, my lord.

HAMLET: How say you then? Would heart of man once think it? But you'll be secret?

HORATIO/BERNARDO: Ay, by heaven, my lord.

HAMLET: There's never a villain dwelling in all Denmark—but he's an arrant knave.

HORATIO: There needs no ghost, my lord, come from the grave, to tell us this.

HAMLET: *(Fighting exhaustion)* Why, right, you are in the right. And so, without more circumstance at all, I hold it fit that we shake hands and part, you, as your business and desire shall point you for every man hath business and desire, such as it is, and for my own poor part, I will go pray.

HORATIO: These are but wild and whirling words, my lord.

HAMLET: I am sorry they offend you heartily. Yes, faith, heartily.

HORATIO: There's no offence, my lord.

HAMLET: Yes, by Saint Patrick, but there is, Horatio! And much offence, too...
And now, good friends, as you are friends, scholars and soldiers, give me one poor request.

HORATIO: What is't, my lord? We will.

HAMLET: Never make known what you have seen tonight.

HORATIO/BERNARDO: My lord, we will not.

HAMLET: Nay, but swear 't.

HORATIO: In faith, my lord, not I.

BERNARDO: Nor I, my lord, in faith.

HAMLET: Upon my sword.

BERNARDO: We have sworn, my lord, already.

DIRECTOR: *(Off)* —Play for time, throw your voice!

HAMLET: Indeed, upon my sword, indeed.

GHOST'S VOICE: *(From under the stage:* HAMLET *ventriloquising the voice)* Swear!

HAMLET: *(An hysterical laugh)* Ha, ha, boy, sayst thou so? Art thou there, truepenny? Come on, you hear this fellow in the cellarage. Consent to swear.

HORATIO: Propose the oath, my lord.

HAMLET: Never to speak of this that you have seen, swear by my sword.

GHOST'S VOICE: *(Below)* Swear!

HAMLET: *Hic et ubique?* Then we'll shift our ground: swear by my sword never to speak of this—

GHOST'S VOICE: *(Below)* Swear by his sword.

HAMLET: Well said, old mole. Canst work i' th' earth so fast? Once more remove, good friends.

HORATIO: O day and night, but this is wondrous strange.

HAMLET: And therefore as a stranger give it welcome. There are more things in heaven and earth, Horatio, than are dreamt of in your philosophy. But come. Here, as before, never, so help you mercy, how strange or odd

some'er I bear myself as I perchance hereafter shall
think meet to put an antic disposition on that you,
at such times seeing me, never shall, with arms
encumbered thus, or this head-shake, or by
pronouncing of some doubtful phrase, as "Well,
well, we know", or "We could an if we would",
or "If we list to speak", or "There be an if they might",
or such ambiguous giving-out, to note that you know
aught of me—this do swear, so grace and mercy at
your most need help you.

GHOST'S VOICE: *(Below)* Swear...

HAMLET: *(Exhaustion)* Rest, rest, perturbéd spirit.
—So, gentlemen, with all my love I do commend me
to you, and what so poor a man as Hamlet is may do t'
express his love and friending to you, God willing, shall
not lack. Let us go in together, and still your fingers on
your lips, I pray.

(They start off. Pause. HAMLET looks back.)

HAMLET: The time is out of joint. O cursèd spite that
ever I was born to set it right! Nay, come, let's go
together.

*(The three move upstage into the dawn, their arms around
each other. They pause for HAMLET to look back over
his shoulder again, to where the Ghost had been. Then,
they disappear. Silence...)*

(DIRECTOR comes on stage.)

DIRECTOR: Five minutes, folks.

(The company circulates, talks, drinks tea, etc.)

*(DIRECTOR and STAGE MANAGER position furniture
elements for Act Two.).*

*(HAMLET and LAERTES rehearse their fencing match under
the tutelage of ACTOR 4.)*

DIRECTOR: May I see Reynaldo, Polonius and Ophelia, please. I want to set the Act Two opening tableau.... So—Polonius, you're sitting on the element, here, on *(Platform)* "One". Reynaldo, you are here, at the boss's left knee—kneeling, of course—and Ophelia you are sitting on Daddy's other knee, and he is, ah, combing your hair... Let me look at this... *(To the technical booth)* Can we have the Act Two pre-set, please.

ASSISTANT STAGE MANAGER: Quiet, please. Act Two beginners, please.

DIRECTOR: *(To the booth)* Good.

ASSISTANT STAGE MANAGER: House lights down and out.... Places...

(Shakespeare's Act Two, Scene One)

DIRECTOR: This is the choreography of "sexpionage", now: stroking his daughter's hair with the comb, A; B, he's pouring poison into his young spy's ear; and, C, seducing both of them vocally. Polonius pours on the poison and the power; Ophelia looks out straight ahead into the past; the spy licks up and picks up the crumbs.

(He nods to ASSISTANT STAGE MANAGER.*)*

ASSISTANT STAGE MANAGER: Curtain up.

POLONIUS: Give him this money and these notes, Reynaldo.

REYNALDO: I will, my lord.

DIRECTOR: *(Off)* Good. Tickle him with the money, have fun—while you play with her hair at the same time. That's it. Go on. It's not sex, it's pseudo-sex, it's Power. Show them your power. Go on.

POLONIUS: ...Ah, take you, as 'twere some distant knowledge of him, as thus: "I know his father and his friends and, in part, him". Do you mark this, Reynaldo?

REYNALDO: Ay, very well, my lord.

POLONIUS: "And, in part, him, but", you may say, "not well. But if 't be he I mean, he's very wild, addicted so and so." And there put on him what forgeries you please—

REYNALDO: As gaming, my lord.

POLONIUS: Ay, or drinking, fencing, swearing, quarrelling, drabbing—you may go so far.

(The father tickles the two young people, causing them all to laugh merrily.)

POLONIUS: ...You have me, have you not?

REYNALDO: *(Breathless)* My lord, I have.

POLONIUS: God be wi' you. Fare you well.

REYNALDO: *(Trying to rise)* Good my lord.

POLONIUS: Let him ply his music.

(More tickling and laughter as REYNALDO *dances out and away.* OPHELIA's *laughter grows hysterical and breaks up into racking sobs.)*

POLONIUS: *(Hugging her)* How now, Ophelia, what's the matter?

OPHELIA: O, my lord, my lord, I have been so affrighted!

POLONIUS: With what, i' th' name of God?

(As OPHELIA *confesses,* POLONIUS *strokes her hair, enters into her fantasy as well as the actual scene she paints. Both stare straight out, seeing the memory.)*

(The lights dim slowly to the end of the scene.)

OPHELIA: My lord, as I was sewing in my closet,
Lord Hamlet, with his doublet all unbraced,
No hat upon his head, his stockings fouled,
Ungartered, and down-gyvd to his ankle,

Pale as his shirt, his knees knocking each other,
And with a look so piteous in purport
As if he had been loosed out of hell
To speak of horrors—he comes before me.

(Silence)

POLONIUS: *(Softly)* Mad for thy love?

OPHELIA: *(Pause)* My lord, I do not know.
(She falls asleep)

(Pause. Very slowly, POLONIUS *stands with* OPHELIA *in his arms, as if she were a sleeping child. He stands staring out, murmurs:)*

POLONIUS: This is the very ecstasy of love...
I will go seek the king.
(He walks slowly away into darkness, carrying the child.)

(As they disappear, bright lights come up on Act Two, Scene Two. Flourish sounds; enter KING *and* QUEEN, ROSENCRANTZ *and* GUILDENSTERN, *and attendants.)*

(Sound, off, of court dance music. The KING *and* QUEEN *march out a simple round of changing dance partners with* ROSENCRANTZ *and* GUILDENSTERN.)*

(Shakespeare's Act Two, Scene Two)

*(*KING, QUEEN *and* HAMLET's *hapless "friends",* ROSENCRANTZ *and* GUILDENSTERN, *dance slowly as the royal couple seduce the young men. Music)*

KING: Welcome, dear Rosencrantz and Guildenstern.
Moreover that we much did long to see you.

QUEEN: *(Overlapping)* Good gentlemen, Hamlet hath much talked of you—

KING: *(Overlapping)* —The need we have to use you did provoke our hasty sending—

QUEEN: *(Overlapping)* —And sure I am two men there is not living to whom he more adheres—

GUILDENSTERN & ROSENCRANTZ: —We both obey and
here give up ourselves in the full bent to lay our service
freely at your feet, to be commanded.

KING: Thanks, Rosencrantz and gentle Guildenstern—

QUEEN: Thanks, Guildenstern and gentle Rosencrantz—

(POLONIUS, *alone, hurries in, interrupts the dance and
whispers into the* KING's *ear. The* KING, *then, whispers to
the* QUEEN.)

QUEEN: Guildenstern and gentle Rosencrantz—
I beseech you instantly to visit my too much changèd
son— Go, some of you, and bring these gentleman
where Hamlet is.

(*Courtiers dance off with* ROSENCRANTZ *and*
GUILDENSTERN. *Music, off, continues softly throughout.*)

(POLONIUS *makes the* KING *and* QUEEN *wait, testing his
power.*)

POLONIUS: ...Mmmm...I have—found the cause—
of Hamlet's lunacy.

KING: O, speak of that! That do I long to hear.

(QUEEN *moves to* POLONIUS' *side, magnetised by power.*)

POLONIUS: ...Your noble son is—mad...I have a
daughter (have while she is mine) who, in her duty
and obedience, mark, hath given me this. Now gather
and surmise. (*His sadistic teasing continues as he reads
the scroll.*)
"...To the celestial, and my soul's idol, the most
beautified Ophelia—"
That's an ill phrase, a vile phrase; "beautified" is a
vile phrase. But you shall hear. Thus:
"In her excellent white bosom, these—"

QUEEN: (*Overlapping*) —Came these from Hamlet to her?

POLONIUS: Good madam, stay awhile. I will be faithful.
"Doubt thou the stars are fire, doubt that the sun doth
move, doubt truth to be a liar, but never doubt I love.
O dear Ophelia, I am ill at these numbers. I have not
art to reckon my groans, but that I love thee, most best,
believe it. *Adieu.*
Thine evermore, most dear lady, whilst this machine
is to him, Hamlet."
This, in obedience, hath my daughter shown me,
and more—

(KING *and* POLONIUS *now begin to struggle over control of
the scroll,* QUEEN'S *attention, the plan of action—everything.*

KING: —But how hath she *received* his love?

POLONIUS: What do you think of me?

KING: As of a man—

POLONIUS: I would fain prove so! No, I went round
to work, and my young mistress thus I did bespeak:
"Lord Hamlet is a prince, out of thy star. This must not
be!" ...And he, repelled (a short tale to make) fell into a
sadness, then into a fast, thence to a watch, thence into a
weakness, thence to a lightness, and, by this declension,
into the madness wherein now he raves and all we
mourn for.

(*Pause. The power struggle continues in silence. Finally,*
KING *snatches the scroll away from* POLONIUS, *hits him
over the head with it, and pulls* QUEEN *to him.*)

KING: Do you think 'tis this?

QUEEN: ...It may be, very like...

POLONIUS: Hath there been such a time, that I—

KING: *(Overlapping)* —Not that I know—

POLONIUS: *(Overlapping)* —I will find where truth is hid,
though it—

KING: *(Overlapping)* How may we try it further?

POLONIUS: *(Milks the suspense)* ...You know sometimes he walks four hours together.... Here in the lobby.

QUEEN: So he does indeed.

POLONIUS: *(Playing his last card to retain power)* At such time I'll loose my daughter to him. *(To* KING*)* Be you and I behind an arras then—

KING: *(Overlapping)* We will try it.

*(*HAMLET *enters, from the back of the auditorium, reading a book.)*

QUEEN: But look where sadly the poor wretch comes reading.

POLONIUS: Away, I do beseech you both, away.
I'll board him presently.
O, give me leave.

(He hurries KING *and* QUEEN *off.)*

POLONIUS: How does my good lord Hamlet?

HAMLET: Well, God-a-mercy.

POLONIUS: *(Pause)* Do you know me, my lord?

HAMLET: *(Sniffing the air)* Excellent well; you are a fishmonger.

POLONIUS: Not I, my lord.

HAMLET: Then I would you were so honest a man.

POLONIUS: Honest, my lord.

HAMLET: Ay, sir. To be honest as this world goes, is to be one man picked out of ten thousand. *(He scans the shadows, looking for spies.)*

POLONIUS: That's very true, my lord.

HAMLET: *(Holds his nose)* For if the sun breed maggots in a dead dog, being a god kissing carrion—have you a daughter?

POLONIUS: I have, my lord.

HAMLET: Let her not walk i' th' sun. Conception is a blessing, but, not as your daughter may conceive, friend, look to 't.

*(*POLONIUS *mutters to the* KING, *hidden in the dark.* HAMLET *takes note of course.)*

POLONIUS: ...Still harping on my daughter. —What do you read, my lord?

HAMLET: Words, words, words.

POLONIUS: What is the matter, my lord?

HAMLET: Between who?

POLONIUS: I mean the matter that you read, my lord.

HAMLET: Slanders, sir; for the satirical rogue says here that old men have grey beards, that their faces are wrinkled, their eyes purging thick amber and plum-tree gum and that they have a plentiful lack of wit, together with most weak hams— *(He roams into the shadows, speaking for* KING'*s benefit, or any of his surveillance.)* —All of which, sir, though I most powerfully and potently believe, yet I hold it not honesty to have it thus set down; for yourself, sir, shall grow old as I am, if like a crab you could go backward.

POLONIUS: *(In shadows)* Though this be madness, yet there is method in 't. —Will you walk out of the air, my lord?

HAMLET: Into my grave?

POLONIUS: *(In shadows)* Indeed, that's out of the air... I will leave him and suddenly contrive the means of

meeting between him and my daughter. —My lord,
I will take my leave of you.

HAMLET: You cannot, sir, take from me anything that
I will more willingly part withal—except my life, except
my life, except my life.

POLONIUS: Fare you well, my lord.

HAMLET: *(In shadows)* These tedious old fools.

(Enter GUILDENSTERN *and* ROSENCRANTZ.*)*

POLONIUS: You go to seek the Lord Hamlet...there he is.

*(*POLONIUS *pretends to exit, but hides and listens—
and* HAMLET *observes this.)*

GUILDENSTERN: God save you, sir. *(To* HAMLET*)*
My honoured lord.

ROSENCRANTZ: My most dear lord.

DIRECTOR: *(Off)* Hamlet—make sure that they know
that you know—and speak to all the spies, royal and
otherwise, and make these "Day Boys" follow you in
and out of the nooks and crannies of this asylum for the
criminally insane.

(Now, HAMLET *leads his "friends" on a tour of the deep
shadows; even down into the aisles of the auditorium among
the hidden and listening audience members.)*

HAMLET: *(Escorting them)* My excellent good friends!
How dost thou, Guildenstern? Ah, Rosencrantz! Good
lads, how do you both?

GUILDENSTERN: *(Laughing)* On Fortune's cap, we are not
the very button.

HAMLET: *(Laughing and leading)* Then you live about her
waist, or in the middle of her favours.

GUILDENSTERN: *(All laughing)* Faith, her privates we.

HAMLET: In the secret parts of Fortune? O, most true! She is a strumpet.... What news?

(They stop.)

ROSENCRANTZ: ...None, my lord, but that the world's grown honest.

*(*HAMLET *stares at the poor pawns. Then, he leads them apart, where they cannot be overheard if they speak in guarded tones.)*

HAMLET: ...Then is doomsday near. But your news is not true.... What have you, my good friends, deserved at the hands of Fortune that she sends you to prison hither?

GUILDENSTERN: ...Prison, my lord?

HAMLET: Shh—Denmark's a prison.

ROSENCRANTZ: *(Whispers)* Then is the world one.

DIRECTOR: *(Off)* Find a safer place. Take pity on them. Try to save them. They're dead and they don't know it. —Again:

*(*ROSENCRANTZ *repeats his speech)*

HAMLET: ...A goodly one, in which there are many confines, wards and dungeons, Denmark being one o' th' worst.

*(*HAMLET *walks and talks with the baffled boys. They find a secluded spot. Their tone is intimate. The friends try to hide their fear from* HAMLET.)*

ROSENCRANTZ: We think not so, my lord.

HAMLET: Why, then, 'tis none to you, for there is nothing either good or bad but thinking makes it so. To me, it is a prison.

ROSENCRANTZ: Why, then, your *ambition* makes it one. 'Tis too *narrow* for your mind.

HAMLET: *(Overlapping)* O God, I could be bounded in
a nutshell and count myself a king of infinite space,
were it not that I have bad dreams.

(Silence. The boys have been shaken by HAMLET'*s pain.
Then:)*

DIRECTOR: *(Off)* Yes. You're moved by the Prince—
and frightened.... Which one of you sniffed, before?

GUILDENSTERN: Me.

DIRECTOR: Good. Keep it in and blow your nose.

GUILDENSTERN: Seriously?

DIRECTOR: Yes! ...So—go back to "bad dreams", and cue
the Gravediggers. You there?

TWO VOICES: *(Off)* Ay!

DIRECTOR: Go.

HAMLET: O God, I could be bounded in a nutshell and
count myself a king of infinite space, were it not that
I have bad dreams.

(Silence. GUILDENSTERN *blows his nose. Then, out of the
silence, in the distance can be heard two voices singing.)*

(The singers are an older and younger man. They are the two
GRAVEDIGGERS/*"Clowns" who we will not see until near
the end of the play.)*

(We hear them, now, drawing closer, then further away.)

GRAVEDIGGERS *(Off)* "...In youth when I did love,
did love, methought it was very sweet to contract—
o—the time for—a—my behove, O, methought there—
a—was nothing—a—meet."

(The voices fade. Silence again. HAMLET *hums the tune he
has just heard, in the distance. Then, dancing slowly...)*

HAMLET: ...Shall we to th' court? For, by my fay,
I cannot reason.

(HAMLET *hops ahead, leading* ROSENCRANTZ *and*
GUILDENSTERN *back up onto the stage, onto a platform.
As they return, several prying heads can be seen ducking
out of sight. The friends dog his heels until* HAMLET *turns
on them. His voice drills low and deep. The lads hang their
heads in shame.)*

HAMLET: ... In the beaten way of friendship—what
make you at Elsinore?

ROSENCRANTZ: T-t-to visit you, my—

HAMLET: Were you not sent for? Is it your own
inclining? —Is it a free visitation? Come, come, deal
justly with me. Come, come—

(GUILDENSTERN *gags.)*

HAMLET: Nay, speak.

(ROSENCRANTZ *and* GUILDENSTERN *are red and white with
shame and nausea.)*

DIRECTOR: *(Off)* More spies, please...thank you.

(More spying heads protrude from the curtains, etc.)

GUILDENSTERN: My lord... *(Whisper)* We were sent for.

(HAMLET *is moved deeply by* ROSENCRANTZ *and*
GUILDENSTERNs' *plight. He puts his arms around their
shoulders. He speaks up and out with great intensity,
the two courtiers huddle under the protecting embrace.)*

HAMLET: I will tell you why; so shall my anticipation
prevent your discovery, and your secrecy to the King
and Queen moult no feather.

(More listening heads appear. HAMLET *fights his despair in
ringing tones.)*

HAMLET: ...I have of late, but wherefore I know not,
lost all my mirth, foregone all custom of exercises,
and, indeed, it goes so heavily with my disposition
that this goodly frame, the earth, seems to me a sterile

promontory; this most excellent canopy, the air,
look you—

(*All the spying heads scan and look.*)

HAMLET: ...This brave o'erhanging firmament,
this majestical roof, fretted with golden fire—why,
it appeareth nothing to me but a foul and pestilent
congregation of vapours. What a piece of work is a
man, how noble in reason, how infinite in faculties,
in form and moving how express and admirable;
in action how like an angel, in apprehension how like
a god: the beauty of the world, the paragon of animals—
and yet to me, what is this quintessence of dust?
Man delights not me—

(HAMLET *spins around—the spy heads disappear—then
turns back to the boys.*)

HAMLET: —No, nor women neither, though by your
smiling you seem to say so.

ROSENCRANTZ: No, my lord—

HAMLET: Why did you laugh then when I said,
"Man delights not me"?

ROSENCRANTZ: To think, my lord, if you delight not
in man, what lenten entertainment the players shall
receive from you.

(HAMLET *jumps in the air.*)

ROSENCRANTZ: We coted them on the way—

(*Sound of approaching actors, off, singing and laughing.*
HAMLET *runs toward the sound.*)

HAMLET: He that plays the King—shall be welcome!

(*Players—the entire company—and* POLONIUS *enter.*
HAMLET *plunges into their midst, hugging and kissing.
There is an uproar of greetings and physical dancing and
jigging.*)

(OLD ACTOR—the first player—is played by DIRECTOR.)

HAMLET: You are welcome, masters; welcome all.
—I am glad to see thee well. —Welcome, good friends.
—O my old friend! *(An almost convulsive embrace)* Why
thy face is valanced since I saw thee last. Com'st thou
to beard me in Denmark? What, my "young lady" and
mistress!

(They embrace.)

HAMLET: We'll have a speech straight. Come, give us a
taste of your quality. Come, a passionate speech.

OLD ACTOR: *(Ringing tones)* What speech, my good lord?

*(Much merriment, until the DIRECTOR steps out of character
to work.)*

DIRECTOR: That's it, that's the tremendous release
we need here—this act's a killer! —we need Hamlet's
"family", he needs these people, these are Yorick's
people...—Alright! —Go to the end of the Old Actor's
speech—we have to work on the "Rogue and peasant
slave" soliloquy. *(To HAMLET)* Have some water.
Don't force your voice.

*(HAMLET drinks water; DIRECTOR relates to the "players",
then resumes his role as OLD ACTOR.)*

(The company take their places for the end of the scene.)

*(The first actor [DIRECTOR] concludes his oration with an
oceanic passion that leaves HAMLET bowled over.)*

OLD ACTOR: ...But if the gods themselves did see
Hecuba when she saw Pyrrhus make malicious sport
in mincing with his sword her husband's limbs, the
instant burst of clamour that she made (unless things
mortal move them not at all), would have made milch
the burning eyes of heaven, and passion in the gods!

(Silence)

POLONIUS: ...Look whe'er he has not turned his colour and has tears in his eyes. Prithee, no more.

(HAMLET *breathes deeply in order to regain control of himself.*)

HAMLET: *(To* OLD ACTOR*)* 'Tis well... *(To* POLONIUS*)* Good my lord, will you see the players well bestowed? Do you hear, let them be well used, for they are the abstract and brief chronicles of the time ...

POLONIUS: *(Pause)* My lord, I will use them according to their desert.

HAMLET: God's bodykins, man, much better! Use every man after his desert and who shall 'scape whipping? Use them after your own honour and dignity... Take them in.

POLONIUS: ...Come, sirs.

HAMLET: Follow him, friends. We'll hear a play tomorrow.

(HAMLET *detains* OLD ACTOR *and the others leave. Their tone is confidential.*)

HAMLET: Dost thou hear me, old friend? Can you play *The Murder of Gonzago?*

OLD ACTOR: Ay, my lord.

HAMLET: We'll ha't tomorrow night. You could, for a need, study a speech of some dozen or sixteen lines, which I would set down and insert in't, could you not?

OLD ACTOR: *(Pause)* ...Ay, my lord.

HAMLET: ...Very well. Follow that lord—and look you, *(Finger on lips)* mock him not.

(OLD ACTOR *exits, leaving a costume and prop basket behind.* HAMLET *opens the treasure trove of old props and costume pieces.*)

(The DIRECTOR *returns, no longer playing the* OLD ACTOR, *and watches from down stage. Then:)*

DIRECTOR: That's it. Take your time. Lose yourself.

*(*HAMLET *is lost in the world of the magic basket. Like a happy child he begins to touch and hold the contents.)*

HAMLET: *(To himself)* ...Now—I am alone... *(He tries on a toy crown. Then laughs at a fool's cap, and puts it on. Smiles and sings to himself. Next, a painted sword and shield is brandished. He stands and begins to imitate the delivery of* OLD ACTOR's *speech.)* "...But if the gods themselves did see Hecuba when she saw Pyrrhus make malicious sport, in mincing, with his sword her husband's limbs— " *(He laughs and hugs himself with joy. With his uncanny imitation of the grand and passionate style of* OLD ACTOR, *he has moved himself deeply. But then, slowly, he remembers where he is and what he is doing. Turns to look for eavesdroppers, gives out a groaning sob.)*
—Ahhhh—hahh... *(He throws down his costume piece and props and begins to pace and curse:)*
...What a rogue and peasant slave am I!
Is it not monstrous that this player here,
But in a fiction, in a dream of passion,
Could force his soul so to his own conceit
That from her working all his visage wann'd,
Tears in his eyes, distraction in his aspect,
A broken voice, and his whole function suiting
With forms to his conceit? —and all for nothing!
For Hecuba!

DIRECTOR: *(Off)* —Let the rhetoric take over—start "Acting" again—how would the Old Actor do it? Hamlet gets drunk again on "Acting", then, the Prince sobers up with guilt, again—the rollercoaster! Hamlet's the Actor—The Prince is the critic! Go!

HAMLET: ...What would he do,
Had he the motive and the cue for passion

That I have? He would drown the stage with tears
And cleave the general ear with horrid speech—
*(He begins, now, to stalk his gaolers and spies. He moves
with stealth along the walls and among curtains. Shouting at
a moving curtain)* Am I a coward?! *(Pause)* Who calls me
"villain"? *(Listens to the echo. Stalking a "rat")* Who does
me this? Ha!

(Something scuttles away, HAMLET *listens to the retreating
steps. Silence. Then:)*

DIRECTOR: *(Off)* Right! You've terrified *them!* Feel your
power, now, go for the kill! The curtains are moving,
the rats are running, the King's *right there*, behind that
curtain! Kill him, kill him now! Where's your dagger—
where's your sword?! You—have—no—weapon—
you idiot! You fool, you fake, you—find a weapon!
ACT!

*(*HAMLET *sobs, dives into the players' basket and comes out
with a toy dagger. His voice builds to a ringing, shrieking
invective.)*

HAMLET: —Bloody, bawdy villain!
Remorseless, treacherous, lecherous, kindless villain!
Ooooo vengeannnnnnce!
*(His prolonged scream on "O vengeance!" carries him to a
curtain. He hurls himself, stabbing, into the darkness. There
is no-one there... He sprawls on the floor in total frustration.
Then rolls back into the light in a frenzy of humiliation)*

DIRECTOR: *(Off)* Now the Critic!

HAMLET: Why, what an ass am I! This is most brave,
That I, the son of a dear father murdered,
Prompted to my revenge by heaven and hell,
Must, like a whore, unpack my heart with words
And fall a-cursing like a very *drab*,
A *scullion! (He gags and retches)*
Fie upon't! Foh!

(He lies flat, panting. Then, slowly, he changes back, again, into an actor in a play!)

DIRECTOR: *(Off)* Now the Actor!

HAMLET: About, my brains! —Hum, I have heard
That guilty creatures sitting at a play
Have, by the very cunning of the scene—

(The prince/actor rises, now reborn as actor—director—playwright.)

HAMLET: ...Been struck so to the soul that presently
They have proclaimed their malefactions.
For murder, though it have no tongue, will speak
With most miraculous organ.

(The Prince is consumed by his scenario, transported and seized by his fantasy. So much so, that he is unaware of the spying heads once again, peeping and peering out of their holes.)

HAMLET: ...I'll have these players
Play something like the murder of my father
Before mine uncle. I'll observe his looks;
I'll tent him to the quick— Ahh! —Ahh!
(Again, he begins to stab and lunge in a kind of slow motion—acting and vocalising both villain and revenger... But, then, once more, he returns to his total isolation.)
...If he do blench,
I know my course! ...This spirit that I have seen
May be the devil, and the devil hath power
T' assume a pleasing shape; yea, and
Perhaps out of my weakness and my melancholy,
He abuses me to damn me.
(One last forlorn attempt to re-enter and hide in the fantasy of the play.) ...I'll have grounds more relative than this.
(Sotto voce) The play...
The play's the thing wherein I'll catch the conscience
of the King!

(HAMLET *calls out his haunting, hollow challenge. He stands, immobile, like a statue of longing. Silence*)

DIRECTOR: *(Off)* ...Hold it. And the spy heads pull back.... Silence: Lights to black... And take a ten minute break, please...

(House lights up)

END OF ACT ONE

ACT TWO

(DIRECTOR *and* STAGE MANAGER *set up for Act Three of Shakespeare's* HAMLET.)

(HAMLET *and* LAERTES *rehearse their duel. Off, the two* GRAVEDIGGERS *practise their songs. At length,* DIRECTOR *blows his whistle.*)

ASSISTANT STAGE MANAGER: Act Three, please—stand by... Act Three beginners, please.

(*Shakespeare's Act Three, Scene One*)

(HAMLET *enters, wearing one of the Actors' robes. He stops to listen, hears voices; hides behind a curtain or wall-flat. From his vantage point, unseen, he watches as* POLONIUS, OPHELIA, KING *hurry on, talking.*)

POLONIUS: Ophelia, read on this prayer book. That show of such an exercise may colour your loneliness.

(*The three mount a platform.* KING *and* POLONIUS *work on* OPHELIA. POLONIUS *positions his daughter and her Holy Book.*)

(KING *attends to the hang of her gown, hair, drapery of her bosom and ensemble.* POLONIUS, *too, joins in—touching, adjusting—and he provides her with a bundle of love letters.*)

(HAMLET, *hidden, watches, appalled at this spectacle of abuse.*)

(HAMLET *starts to stagger away, but is heard by the two men.*)

POLONIUS: I hear him coming. Let's withdraw, my lord.

(POLONIUS *and Claudius secrete themselves behind an opposite curtain. Again,* HAMLET *sees the entire action.)*

(OPHELIA *holds her prayerful pose, but her prayer book is upside down.)*

(Silence. HAMLET *is paralysed. Torn. He starts to leave. Stops. Finally, returns to* OPHELIA)

HAMLET: ... Nymph, in thy orisons
Be all my sins remembered.

(The prince stands below OPHELIA's *platform, looking up at her. She cannot meet his gaze; she looks down; adjusts her book, then holds out the bundle of love letters.)*

(There is a palpable sadness between them: bound together yet forever parted.)

OPHELIA: My lord, I have remembrances of yours,
That I have longèd long to re-deliver.
I pray you now receive them.

(HAMLET *takes the letters, glances through them. Heaves a deep sigh. Hands them back to* OPHELIA.)

HAMLET: ...No, not I. I never gave you aught.

OPHELIA: *(Pause)* ...My honoured lord, you know right well you did.

HAMLET: —Ha, ha, are you honest?

OPHELIA: My lord?

(HAMLET *is drawn to* OPHELIA, *he has to mount her platform. He touches her, she reacts. He touches her again. When he speaks there is a lump in his throat.)*

HAMLET: ...Are you fair?

(The two lovers are both breathless.)

OPHELIA: What means your lordship?

(He touches her again. He drops his voice so as not to be overheard.)

HAMLET: ...I did love you once.

(OPHELIA's hand jerks out—out of her control—to touch HAMLET. Then, she moves into his arms.)

OPHELIA: Indeed, my lord, you made me believe so.

(HAMLET kisses OPHELIA deeply. His voice is tender, despite his words.)

HAMLET: You should not have believed me....

(Their embrace becomes compulsive as they kiss hungrily.)

(The lovers are almost beyond control, when from the curtains two heads pop out: KING and POLONIUS.)

(HAMLET's reaction is instant fury. He leaps from the platform, toward the spies, bellowing:)

HAMLET: I loved you not!

(OPHELIA sobs out a few words, but the prince is beside himself: he lashes her with his voice and words, and KING and POLONIUS as well.)

(However, when HAMLET leaps into the curtains, screaming—again, there is no-one there. So, he rounds on OPHELIA, again, and then runs back into the draperies cursing, still looking for the royal spies.)

HAMLET: —Get thee to a nunnery. Why would'st thou be a breeder of sinners? I am myself indifferent honest, but yet I could accuse me of such things that it were better my *mother (Looking for the KING)* had not borne me—

(OPHELIA collapses to her knees. HAMLET turns back to attack her but, sobbing through his rage we can hear his utter despair.)

HAMLET: —What should such fellows as I do crawling between earth and heaven?
(He whirls furiously toward the shadows:)
We are arrant knaves, all; believe none of us. Go thy ways to a nunnery!

(OPHELIA loses consciousness. Silence. HAMLET, stunned, kneels over her. He lifts her in his arms. He is hoarse, almost spent.)

HAMLET: ...Where's your father?

(OPHELIA opens her eyes. She lies in HAMLET's arms. His eyes plead with her—to be loyal, to love him.)

(OPHELIA is on the rack. This is the choice of her lifetime. Whom should she betray? They have ripped her apart.)

OPHELIA: ...At home...my lord.

(OPHELIA's tortured lie is fatal to them both. They shake in each other's arms.)

(HAMLET slowly separates himself and tries to stand. He trembles and pants like a wounded beast.)

HAMLET: ...Let the doors be shut upon him...that he may play the fool nowhere but in's own house...

(HAMLET makes to leave but stumbles to his knees. On all fours he tries to crawl away. OPHELIA shrieks out in pain:)

OPHELIA: O, help him, you sweet heavens!

(OPHELIA runs to help HAMLET; he fights her off; rises to his knees; croaks his curse into her body as he clings to her waist for balance.)

HAMLET: I have heard of your paintings too, well enough. God hath given you one face, and you make yourself another...you jig and amble, and you lisp... Go to, I'll no more on't. *It hath made me mad!*

(HAMLET's *trembling is now a series of almost epileptic twitches and spasms. There can be no question but that he is near a complete breakdown.*)

(OPHELIA *is terrified to the point of loss of control and continence. Her whimpers, cries and groans underscore* HAMLET's *vomit-like curse.*)

HAMLET: —I say we will have no more marriages. Those that are married already—all but *one!* —shall live. The rest shall keep as they are. (*He starts to crawl away.*) To a nunnery, go!...

(OPHELIA *watches, in horror, as the prince crawls very slowly into the deep shadows.*)

(*Then a terrible sight:* OPHELIA, *as if in a nightmare, sinks to her knees, and she, too, begins to crawl after her lover—some ten feet or so behind.*)

(*But* HAMLET *reaches the dark edge of the space and disappears, leaving* OPHELIA *alone.*)

(*At this,* POLONIUS *and* KING *slink in. They pick up* OPHELIA. *She cannot stand. They support her; walk her off slowly as they talk in hushed tones.*)

POLONIUS: How now, Ophelia? ...You need not tell us what Lord Hamlet said. We heard it all. —My lord, if you hold it fit, after the play, let his Queen-Mother all alone entreat him to show his grief. Let her be round with him; and I'll be placed, so please you, in the ear of all their conference.

(*The two men take turns almost dragging* OPHELIA *off.*)

POLONIUS: ...If she find him not, to England send him, or confine him where your wisdom best shall think...

KING: ...It shall be so. Madness in great ones must not unwatched go.

(*And they are gone. The stage is empty except for several heads watching from the darkness.*)

(The DIRECTOR *returns from the wings.)*

DIRECTOR: Right—what's the time? *(He studies his watch, then says something privately to the* STAGE MANAGER.*)* ...Can we have some lights. —Thank you... Now—very strong. New dimensions. I'm starting to believe in this Soulbreaker of a Prison! So—what I want is to skip to the end of the mousetrap scene—after the play within the play—to the King's prayer, and, then, the closet scene. Then, bits and pieces of Act Four, as far as "Do it England..." Then—we go to Act Five and work the Graveyard Scene, and then—we go home... All clear?

(A chorus of "no"; nervous complaints and jokes.)

DIRECTOR: Then, tomorrow, we pick up all the missed scenes we're skipping today... Trust me, alright? Thank you, stand by...let's see the Ghost Special, please.

(The DIRECTOR *buckles on a prop sword and swordbelt and prepares to play the* KING's *prayer scene.)*

(The only light is the "Ghost Special".)

(Shakespeare's Act Three, Scene Three)

DIRECTOR: ...Can you, ah, take it down a point... And open the "barndoor" a little—that's good, I think?

SSTAGE MANAGER: I think so.

DIRECTOR: Let's try it...I want to take it from the entrance, then we'll see. Can we have the *furore* of the castle, please.

(The STAGE MANAGER *cues and leads the company in a sound-scape of off-stage reaction to the debacle of the scene just past, the play within the play, or "mousetrap" scene.)*

STAGE MANAGER & COMPANY: Ready? Stage Right, Go! — "He poisons him in the garden for his estate / He poisons him— " Stage Left, Go! — "His name's Gonzago— " / "He poisons him" / "Poisons him" /

"His name" / "His name" / "His name" / "Gonzago"
/ "Gonzago" / "Gonzago" ...

*(Thus, the overlapping dialogue from the previous
scene—combined with shrieks, curses, cries and
whispers—create an aural environment for a castle
in conflict.)*

(As KING's *prayer scene progresses the sounds of political
and personal turmoil fade out, replaced by a dead midnight
silence that is broken only by the tolling church bells.)*

(Now, DIRECTOR *enters as* KING. *He strides in and across
the stage but is stopped in his tracks by the sudden presence
of a distant beam of light: the "Ghost Special".)*

*(*KING *stops, stares—then appears to listen and see someone
or something. As he speaks and plays the scene with the beam
of light, we deduce that now he, too, sees and hears the
Ghost!)*

*(*KING's *voice and body make a savage mockery of the Ghost's
unheard accusations.)*

KING: *(As if responding)* Ohhhh— *(As if repeating)* My
offence is rank, it smells to heaven; it hath the primal
eldest curse upon't. A brother's murder? —Pray can
I not! ... *(He now launches into a fierce justification of his
entire life—as the far superior but younger brother [!])*
What if this cursèd hand were thicker than itself with
brother's blood? Is there not rain enough in the sweet
heavens to wash it white as snow? *(The argument rages.
He laughs and curses.)* — "Forgive me my foul murder"?!
(A savage laugh) That cannot be, since I am still
"possessed" of those effects for which I *did* the murder:
*(A complete soul-bargaining confrontation with his Brother
or God or both of them:)* My crown! *(Puts crown on floor)*
—Mine own ambition! *(Unbuckles sword and belt, puts
aside on floor)* —My Queen! *(He starts to take off his
robe—then wraps it more closely than ever around himself;
and squares off, ready to fight to the finish—)*

KING: (DIRECTOR) Line?

STAGE MANAGER: "What then?"

DIRECTOR: Is this working?

STAGE MANAGER: Keep the focus on your brother—
on the Ghost—then if he changes into "God", so be it,
the audience'll get it.

KING: —What then?! What rests?! Try what repentance
can. What can it not?
Yet what can it, when one cannot repent?! *(Panting)*
Help, angels! Make assay... Bow, stubborn knees, and
heart with strings of steel... *(He goes down like a bull in
the slaughter. And his "prayer" is one prolonged and vicious
curse. A mantra of envy, jealousy, rationalisation and
unreconstructed revenge and resentment.)*

*(This muttered, spitting word-salad of revolt and rejection
explains why* KING *does not hear* HAMLET's *low vows when
the prince enters.)*

(The only words from the text that HAMLET *and the
audience can make out, as* KING *"prays", are such as below,
and all of them apply to the tyranny of his older brother,
the Ghost:)*

KING: ...Wretched state! ...Bosom black as death!
...Corrupted currents of this world! ...Offence's gilded
hand! ...Like a man to double-business bound!...

(Meanwhile, HAMLET *crosses far up stage of the kneeling,
seething regicide. He stops to hear.)*

KING: ...Shove by justice... *(A low laugh)* The wicked
prize itself buys out the law! *(Laugh)* No shuffling there
(Laughs) Ahh—limèd soul...

*(The prince hears parts of the above even as he, too, pours out
his conflicted impulses. Slurring his words, his voice hoarse
and resonant with extreme agitation and exhaustion.)*

HAMLET: ...Now might I do it pat, now he is praying...

(But, again, HAMLET *has no weapon! Then, he spies the*
KING's *sword and sword belt, spread just behind the kneeling*
Claudius. HAMLET *moves down, like a cat, to steal the*
weapon.

HAMLET: ...And now I'll do it. *(He has the sword)*
...That would be scann'd...

(HAMLET *pauses, shackled by ambivalence. He rocks from*
side to side, debating with himself—as is KING, *as well:*
it is as if there are four distinct characters, now, trapped
in this midnight scene.)

KING:	HAMLET:
...Compelled, even to the teeth... My stronger guilt...	
	He took my father grossly, full of bread, with all his crimes broad blown, as flush as May...
...I stand in pause...then I'll look up, *(Laughs)* my fault is past!	
	Up sword, and know thou a more horrid hent—when he is drunk asleep, or in his rage—
Whereto serves mercy... this two-fold force *(Spits in disgust)*...	
	Or in the incestuous pleasure of his bed... my mother...stays... this physic but prolongs thy sickly days. *(Exit with the sword)*

(HAMLET *slips away. Claudius concludes as he began,
enraged. He glares up at his "brother"—the Ghost Special.*

KING: —My words fly up, my thoughts remain below...
(*Still on his knees, he reaches behind him for his sword.
Not there. Tries the other side. No!*)

(*Claudius arches in terror; stares up at the Ghost/God beam,
then scrambles like a big bug, stabbing about for his missing
weapon. Finally, he freezes. Stares back at the beam of light.*)

(*The Ghost Special fades slowly to black as the church bells
toll midnight.*)

(*Shakespeare's Act Three, Scene Four*)

(*Church bells toll. Lights up on* QUEEN's *bedroom area.
Elements for the bed and seats; draperies; a tall portable
mirror. And a large tapestry that pictures the late King
Hamlet in a famous battle scene on the ice! "The Victory
Over Norway!"*)

(HAMLET *can be heard calling from a dark corridor
somewhere in the castle.*)

HAMLET: (*Off*) Mother!

(QUEEN's *bedroom, however, is empty and there is no
answer. Silence*)

HAMLET: (*Off, closer*) Mother?

(*A round of scurrying footsteps. Pause. Then, again. A spy
materialises out of the darkness, slips into* QUEEN's *bedroom,
and, finding it empty, he slips away, back into the darkness.*)

(*Silence. Then more footsteps. Out of the darkness* HAMLET
appears. He still carries the KING's *sword. Yet, once again,
his mood has shifted radically. He is, clearly, exhausted—
almost dragging the weapon, as a boy would his father's
sword.*)

(*The tremendous highs and lows of the past twenty-four
hours seem to have aged* HAMLET, *giving him the skeletal*

body image of an old man, or a crippled child. His voice, too, is almost gone now.)

(Like a spent runner HAMLET *halts in the light spilling from his mother's bedroom. He stands on the threshold, looking, waiting.)*

HAMLET: ...Mother... *(He waits. Silence. He sways, almost unconscious on his feet. At length, he turns away, takes two steps. Stops. Turns back and, this time, enters the chamber.)*

DIRECTOR *(Off)* See yourself in the mirror. Who are you?

(Inside, HAMLET *stares into the mirror. His head sinks, then snaps up, sinks again—forcing him to move to stay awake.)*

*(*HAMLET *begins an unsteady tour of the room. Stops in front of the hanging war tableau of his father's famous victory. Silence, then church bells toll the half-hour.)*

*(*HAMLET *drops his mesmerized gaze from the vainglorious scene pictured on the large tapestry. He stumbles over to the bed and sinks down, murmuring—)*

HAMLET: ...Mother...

(And, at last, HAMLET *sleeps. Muttering to himself: a word from the play, "Hecuba", but all the rest is choked and garbled. He thrashes, too, for a time, then the fever seems to pass, and he rests.... Silence as he sleeps, then a few bells, and silence again...)*

(After a time, the "Victory Over Norway" tapestry shivers, and from behind the bloody scene, QUEEN *steps out to behold* HAMLET. *She stands there, breathing, gazing down at his spent figure.)*

HAMLET: *(In his sleep)* ...Mmmm...

(Slowly, QUEEN *moves to the bed and sits down next to the sleeping* HAMLET. *She watches him. Then, strokes his hair, very lightly. And he seems to react slightly. When she brushes his forehead with her lips, the youth definitely leans toward her.)*

(*Still sitting,* QUEEN *circles her arm like a protective shield around her boy's shoulder. They breathe together.*)

(*Are we watching a dream,* HAMLET's *dream, or is this actually happening? The answer to that question is provided by* POLONIUS.)

(OLD SPY *pokes his head out from another hanging curtain and glares at* QUEEN. *And she, the mother, glares back like any animal protecting its own. She tightens her grip around the sleeping prince's shoulder.*)

(HAMLET *stirs,* POLONIUS *withdraws.* QUEEN *looks down, into* HAMLET's *open eyes. Slowly, he wakes up to where he is. His voice is as soft as a child's.*

HAMLET: ...Mother...

(QUEEN *seems about to speak. As she bends over* HAMLET, POLONIUS, *again, shows his head. His protruding eyes warn her. She stiffens.* HAMLET—*who cannot see* OLD SPY's *head wagging out from the curtain behind him*—*reacts to his mother's sudden change of breathing and posture.*)

HAMLET: ...What's the matter?

QUEEN: Hamlet...

(HAMLET *fixes on* QUEEN's *face. She seems about to blurt out a terrible truth. But the prime minister's eyes pronounce the death sentence, should she forget herself at this moment of crisis.*)

(QUEEN's *head bows, at last, in submission.* HAMLET, *painfully awake now, turns to look behind him, but there is no-one there. Are the drapes moving slightly?*)

(*A jolt of fear and rage shocks* HAMLET *to his feet. Sword in hand he moves like a tiger toward the black drapery.*)

QUEEN: Hamlet! Thou hast thy father much offended!

(QUEEN *is up—her voice a whip of warning.* HAMLET *stares back at her, his sword poised—to kill someone!*)

(Then, like a bolt from the blue, QUEEN *points—with her entire body—in warning, toward the curtains that hide the certain death that threatens them both.)*

*(*HAMLET, *sword raised, stands amazed... Then he walks out of the scene.)*

(The actor playing HAMLET *walks out of the set and the scene. Walks to the edge of the stage.)*

DIRECTOR: *(Off)* What's going on?

ACTOR: (HAMLET) That's what I want to know.

(The DIRECTOR *is on the stage, now, and [Actor]* POLONIUS *has come out into the light. The three men are all staring at [*ACTOR*]* QUEEN.)

ACTOR: (QUEEN) "This scene is our big problem" —that's what you said Thursday.

DIRECTOR: *(Pause)* That's true.

ACTOR: (QUEEN) "What would Gertrude do?" —you said— "Do what you would do if you were his mother", you said.

DIRECTOR: *(Pause)* I did.

ACTOR: (QUEEN) "His mother", you said, not "Gertrude", not "the Queen". You said—

DIRECTOR: I said—

ACTOR: (QUEEN) You said "His mother", and that—

DIRECTOR: She's the—

ACTOR: (QUEEN) Listen—if *I* were his

"mother" and I was also the "Queen" —the "Queen Mother" —I would be torn apart because I would have to choose between betraying my son or my husband, and I—

DIRECTOR: But Gertrude chooses to—

ACTOR: (QUEEN) I mean, Polonius says, "tis meet that some more audience than a mother, since nature—

ACTOR: (POLONIUS *joins in*) —makes them partial, should all o'erhear,
The speech, of vantage".

DIRECTOR: I know but the Queen....

ACTOR: (QUEEN) *But his Mother chooses to save her son!*

(All stare at the ACTOR playing the QUEEN.)

ACTOR: (POLONIUS) ...Excuse me—but that would stop the scene.

ACTOR: (HAMLET) *(Pause)* Stop the play.

DIRECTOR: Wait—

ACTOR: (QUEEN) And that is the truth. She stops— the *mother—stops* the farce, the lie: the play within the play within the play.

(Silence. Other actors have now joined those in the QUEEN's bedroom.)

ACTOR: (QUEEN) She tries. That is what she *tries* to do.

DIRECTOR: *(Pause)* And that stops the play.

ACTOR: (QUEEN) That stops the play...she tries. And she fails. And she has to play her role— "Queen Gertrude" —again. She betrays her son. And that starts the rest of the play, again.

(Now, they all stare at DIRECTOR. He begins to walk slowly around the edge of the bedroom area. He circles, they watch.)

DIRECTOR: ...Hamlet says—in Act Four—Hamlet tells the King, "Father and Mother are Man and Wife / Man and Wife are one flesh..."

ACTOR: (QUEEN) I know.

DIRECTOR: That's the "Law".

ACTOR: (QUEEN) That's the "Law" —but it's not the *truth.*

(The DIRECTOR *paces, again. Then:)*

DIRECTOR: Does this mean that she sees the Ghost, too?

ACTOR: (QUEEN) ...I don't know...

DIRECTOR: ...This is huge... Repercussions... Ramifications... As they say— Wow! ...Jesus! ...Let's sleep on it.

(Silence. Then the DIRECTOR *whispers "I love you" in the* ACTOR's *ear and she hugs him—and the company comes back to life.)*

DIRECTOR: Act Four, Scene Three; Polonius is dead, the King confronts Hamlet.

STAGE MANAGER: (QUEEN) Act Four, Scene Three, please: "Now, Hamlet, where's Polonius?"

(Shakespeare's Act Four, Scene Three)

(The company/the court surround KING *as he faces off with* HAMLET.)

KING: Now, Hamlet, where's Polonius?

HAMLET: At supper.

KING: At supper where?

HAMLET: Not where he eats, but where he is eaten. A certain convocation of politic worms are e'en at him.

*(*HAMLET *speaks not only to the* KING *but also gets "up close and personal" with the members of the court.)*

*(*HAMLET *is beyond exhaustion. He has, in fact, a second wind of gallows wit and insight. He strikes* KING *and court as, somehow, older, tougher, much more dangerous. More—king-like?!)*

HAMLET: ...Your worm is your only emperor for diet. We fat all creatures else to fat us, and we fat ourselves for maggots. Your fat King *(In KING's face)* and your lean beggar is but variable service—two dishes but to one table. That's the end.

KING: *(Controlling the court)* Alas, alas!

HAMLET: A man may fish with the worm that hath eat of a king and eat of the fish that hath fed of that worm.

KING: What dost thou mean by this?

HAMLET: Nothing—but to show you how a king may go a progress through the guts of a beggar.

(Silence. The court is dumbfounded. HAMLET starts to leave. No-one moves to stop him. KING is forced to block his way.)

KING: Where—is—Polonius?

HAMLET: In heaven... Send thither to see. If your messenger find him not there seek him i' th' other place yourself. But, indeed, if you find him not within the month, you shall nose him as you go up the stairs into the lobby.

KING: *(To court)* Go, seek him there.

HAMLET: *(Laughing)* He will stay till you come.

(KING moves in to HAMLET. They are face to face.)

KING: Hamlet—prepare thyself. The bark is ready, and everything is bent for England.

HAMLET: *(Overlapping)* For England!

KING: Ay, Hamlet.

HAMLET: Good.

KING: *(Walking away)* So is it, if thou knew'st our purposes.

HAMLET: I see a cherub that sees them. But, come, for England... Farewell, dear mother.

KING: *(Turns)* Thy loving father, Hamlet.

(The prince stares out, while speaking to his mother.)

HAMLET: My mother... Father and mother is man and wife. Man and wife is one flesh, and so, my mother. —*Come, for England!*

(HAMLET races off laughing. KING grabs his testicles, gathers his powers; looks out and up into the old Ghost Special light, and barks out his glottal commands.)

KING: ...Do it, England! For like the hectic in my blood he rages, and thou must cure me! Till I know 'tis done, howe'er my haps, my joys were ne'er begun.

(Lights to black. Then general lighting as KING returns to his directorial role.)

DIRECTOR: Ah, members of the Court: look—remember: in that scene, for the first time, you see that Hamlet could be dangerous—if he goes to the "People". He's wasted, he's running on empty, but there are flashes of "Hamlet the Dane"! —Anyway, remember it's four in the morning and your future depends on when and where and whom you decide to betray or not to betray. —Now, can I see the Act Five, Scene One, people, please.

(HAMLET, HORATIO, and the two GRAVEDIGGERS join DIRECTOR on stage. The elements, or cubicles are adjusted to mark the open grave and/or trap D L.)

(Shakespeare's Act Five, Scene One)

DIRECTOR: *(To the booth)* Can I see late afternoon, late April sunshine, and a lot of birdsong. *(Lights and sound)* ...Good... Now—I would like to see you run this scene first, without a stop, and then we'll work it and then we'll go home. —O K? *(He blows his whistle.)*

Everybody—that's it. Good work. —Tomorrow it's
all costumes and props for a two P M run-through,
no make-up. We'll work the "Closet" scene at ten A M,
then Ophelia mad scenes at eleven-thirty A M. Bring
your lunches, food and water, the lot. There will be
food provided for supper. O K, thank you for a helluva
day and for "stopping the play"... And Wednesday,
full make-up.

STAGE MANAGER: (QUEEN) "Badgered up!"

(Laughter as the company departs. Alone, the DIRECTOR
talks to the actors in the graveyard scene.)

DIRECTOR: *(Walking and talking)* You have it in mind?
By Saturday we'll have the King Hamlet tomb,
"marblejaws" and statue here, up right; Polonius' tomb
will be here, center right. And a scattering of lesser
stones all the way up stage on an acute perspective,
so, for once, the audience will actually see the markers...
What I need from Hamlet and Horatio is the stinging
pungency of the smell, the odour, the ambience of
the open grave. Shakespeare uses smell directly and
indirectly at least five times in this scene. I don't know
what more the man can do to signal the actors that
he's not kidding around about finitude and death, here.
But the actors don't play the stench, even the great
ones. They say the words and the "ughs" and the
"pahs" but they won't play it. And that means the
audience never gets it. They see a few shining skulls,
and a nod to poor Yorick. But that's it. The "Brodie
Notes". *(He helps distribute skulls around the grave.)*
And then, just to make sure the meaning of the play
gets buried they cut the apprentice gravedigger,
the old man's "son", and they cut out all the riddles—
the riddles and puns that add up to nothing less than
the meaning of the entire g'damn work of art.
    Remember—every riddle hides a truth: and the truth
is that they are burying Princess Di, here, today. Right

here. And Hamlet, too, unless you can spring him
from this trap. And Fortinbras and his army are waiting
on the beach—watching... Norway is going to occupy
Denmark. It's over and everybody in little Elsinore
knows it's over... You're an old man now. You came
in with Hamlet and you're going out with him. But,
now, there's your son: save your son, old man, and save
Hamlet—they're all your sons. And they will have to
grow up, "literally", overnight. So let your boy, here,
know that there will be no time for clowning, after
today. *(He climbs down into the grave.)* So, will you, by
God, smell it—it's a very warm spring day and there
are also some sweet scents, too, all the fresh flowers on
the King's grave, and the birdsong. But the aroma of
death rises like a slow tide until the end of the scene.
And in that medium Hamlet finds the answer to his
question—and I don't mean "To be or not to be?"
—Let's go: we want the audience, who think they know
this play, to be absolutely astonished when the "ghost"
of Yorick fills up the stage, and the theatre, and then the
world. *(He climbs up and goes to* HORATIO.*)* You're the
key: you have to try to keep the Prince moving forward
on the Revenge Plot conveyor belt. No detours, no
side-shows, cut the Clowns and their jokes that aren't
funny anyway. It's Ophelia's grave, that's all that
matters. You don't want to go there, and Hamlet might
go nuts, and the Gravedigger's an old drunk, and the
Second Clown doesn't exist, so do not let Hamlet's
curiosity lead him into this stinking, and I mean
stinking, dead end. The dead end where the Narrative
is buried, where Shakespeare's play reaches its nadir
and its apotheosis. Hold your nose, literally, use your
lace handkerchief and get the Prince out of there as
soon as you can. As far as you're concerned you're only
there so that your hero can jump into the grave and
take the piss out of Laertes. Everything else is
clown-show and noise.

(Lights and sound have now set the scene. DIRECTOR *puts his arm around* HORATIO's *shoulder.*

DIRECTOR: Let it happen. Watch your friend, the Prince, and the old Digger, here. The old man also knows where the bodies are buried. The old joker who picks up a skull—without looking at it! —and announces "that this same skull, sir, was Yorick's skull". And then it hits you—that this clown has known who you guys are, all along. That he's been trying to tell you something behind all that horseplay. And, then, you see Hamlet bowled over by the return of Yorick. And then you know—and we know—that this is the end of Shakespeare's Hamlet. The old Revenge Plot goes on forever, but right here the home truth hits you between the eyes: it stops the play: under the mask of the "First Clown", was the wise and weathered phiz of the Old Gravedigger—and under that mask is Yorick—and behind him, at last, is Master William Shakespeare who, alone, knows who's who in this charnel-house. He was there "the day Young Hamlet was born", and he's here today—when the Prince must die: do the math! But what wipes you out is when you see that Hamlet sees all this, too, and a lot more—and that he's happy! Joyful—like the Old Gravedigger. And you're amazed and struck dumb. Because, of course, you don't yet comprehend that Hamlet recognises the Old Clown as none other than—the Ghost of Yorick himself!

(Silence. DIRECTOR, HAMLET, *and* HORATIO *stare at each other.* DIRECTOR *puts a hand on their shoulders. The exchange is quiet and deep.)*

DIRECTOR: Something just hit me..."the old male..."

ACTOR: *(*HAMLET*)* Act One.

DIRECTOR:Remember? And the "pioneer" —in the "cellarage". When Hamlet tells Horatio that his strategy will be to put on "antic disposition on"? And, now, he—

ACTOR: (HAMLET) The jokes, the—

DIRECTOR: What?

ACTOR: (HAMLET) The jokes! (Pause) When Hamlet
takes the micky, when he sends up the Ghost—calls
him an "old mole", for God's sake—I mean, no one's
ever understood how the prince can go from swearing
to the ghost of his father, one minute, that he's going to
give up his youth, his love life, his art, his education—
everything! —for his father, to revenge his head father,
and then—

DIRECTOR: And, then, the next moment, he's calling the
murdered King an "old mole"! That's what—

ACTOR: (HAMLET) That's what I'm—

ACTOR: (OLD GRAVEDIGGER) Taking the piss.

ACTOR: (HAMLET) That's what I'm—

ACTOR: (HORATIO) The "old mole"...

(Pause)

ACTOR: (HAMLET) That's Yorick talking.

DIRECTOR: (Softly) Eureka.

ACTOR: (HAMLET) Not "The Prince".

ACTOR: (OLD GRAVEDIGGER) No.

DIRECTOR: No. Not "The Prince". Not even "Hamlet".

ACTOR: (HAMLET) No...Yorick...

(DIRECTOR embraces the rapt HORATIO and, then,
HAMLET. Then, he exits into the darkness.)

DIRECTOR: Go. No stops.

(The two GRAVEDIGGERS can be heard talking and laughing
as they approach the graveyard: "Beggars and Kings and
worms and beggars and—")

OLD GRAVEDIGGER: *(Off)* ...Ha—ha— Go to! Away, nay—answer me that?

(OLD GRAVEDIGGER, the father, and YOUNG GRAVEDIGGER, the son, enter with spades and other tools of their trade. They stop to cool off, for a moment, before approaching the newly opened grave, down stage.)

DIRECTOR: *(Off)* Father—scan the horizon. You need to warn Hamlet before the funeral procession arrives. And you need to prepare your son, right now, before Fortinbras and his shock troops make their move on the Castle. Sorry, go on.

(They move down to the grave to begin work. Their technique is an economical and complete craftsmanship. OLD GRAVEDIGGER spits into his hands, YOUNG GRAVEDIGGER imitates him. The father hides a smile and picks up the schooling, the teaching, the protecting of the youth. The father scans the approaches to the graveyard, as if he might be expecting someone.)

OLD GRAVEDIGGER: Mmm... Is she to be buried in Christian burial, when she wilfully seeks her own "salvation"?

YOUNG GRAVEDIGGER: I tell thee she is. The crowner hath sat on her and finds it Christian burial.

OLD GRAVEDIGGER: Mm— Hmmm—how can that be, unless she drowned herself in her own defence?

YOUNG GRAVEDIGGER: Why, 'tis found so.

OLD GRAVEDIGGER: It must be se offendendo, it cannot be else. For here lies the point: if I drown myself willingly, it argues an act, and an act hath three branches—it is to act, to do, to perform. Argal, she drowned herself willingly.

YOUNG GRAVEDIGGER: Nay, but hear you—

DIRECTOR: *(Off)* Right—the boy's quick, he's dancing, learning's a game, and learning is loving for this father and child—the only healthy relationship in the entire play—but you have to get through to the lad how to slip past Fortinbras' thugs. Play the game, but warn him!

OLD GRAVEDIGGER: —Give me leave... Here lies the water; good. Here stands the man; good. If the man go to this water and drown himself, it is—will he, nil he—he goes; mark you that. But if the water comes to him, he drowns not himself. Argal, he that is not guilty of his own death shortens not his own life.

(Thus, the logic and law of power, church and state. YOUNG GRAVEDIGGER *is stymied.* OLD GRAVEDIGGER's *catechism is the chop-logic of privilege and, after a frustrated cogitation, the lad sees through the riddle and the rationalization— as he was meant to.)*

YOUNG GRAVEDIGGER: ...But is this the law?

OLD GRAVEDIGGER: Ay, marry, is't—crowner's quest law.

(The son's disgust leads him to the answer that the father was fishing to find.)

YOUNG GRAVEDIGGER: Will you ha' the truth on't? If this had not been a gentlewoman, she would have been buried out of Christian burial!

DIRECTOR: *(Off)* Warn him now!

OLD GRAVEDIGGER: Why, there thou sayst! *(He laughs and dances a little jig with joy, and drives home the warning.)* And the more pity that great folk should have count'nance in this world to hang themselves more than their even-Christian.... *(He scans the roads, again. Then:)* ...Come, my spade... There is no ancient gentleman but gard'ners, ditchers, and grave-makers. They hold up Adam's profession.

YOUNG GRAVEDIGGER: Was he a gentleman?

OLD GRAVEDIGGER: He was the first that ever bore arms.

YOUNG GRAVEDIGGER: Why, he had none.

DIRECTOR: *(Off)* You have to frighten him a bit, now.
You have to remind him who he is—a gravedigger.
And that the Fortinbras of this world come and go—
but we *endure.*

OLD GRAVEDIGGER: What, art a heathen? The scripture
says "Adam digged". Could he dig without arms?
...I'll put another question to thee. If thou answerest
me not to the purpose, confess thyself—

DIRECTOR: *(Off)* Good. Getting scared. We're the First
and the Last. This is deadly serious, now there's a
shit-storm coming.

YOUNG GRAVEDIGGER: Go to!

OLD GRAVEDIGGER: *(Softly, seriously)* What is he that
builds stronger than either the mason, the shipwright,
or the carpenter?

*(*YOUNG GRAVEDIGGER *looks up into* OLD
GRAVEDIGGER's *face, catching his tone and drift.)*

YOUNG GRAVEDIGGER: ...Marry—now I can tell...

OLD GRAVEDIGGER: *(Face to face)* To't.

YOUNG GRAVEDIGGER *(Straining)* ...Mass, I cannot tell.

(Now, over the youth's shoulder, the father sees HAMLET *and*
HORATIO *in the distance.)*

(The father embraces the son; plants the answer in his ear.)

OLD GRAVEDIGGER: ...Cudgel thy brains no more about
it...and when you are asked this question next, say "A
grave-maker". The houses he makes last till doomsday.
(Watching HAMLET's *approach)* Go, get thee in, and fetch
me a stoup of liquor.

(YOUNG GRAVEDIGGER *trots off, never seeing* HAMLET *and* HORATIO *as they draw near.*)

(OLD GRAVEDIGGER *feigns ignorance of the prince's presence, by beginning to dig and singing a song.*)

(*Meanwhile,* HAMLET *and* HORATIO *have reached the grave area. Each holds a handkerchief to his nose.* HORATIO *attempts to walk past as quickly as possible, but* HAMLET *stops.*)

OLD GRAVEDIGGER: (*Sings*)
In youth when I did love, did love,
Methought it was very sweet
To contract-o-the time for-a-my behove,
O, methought there-a-was nothing-a-meet.

HAMLET: Has this fellow no feeling of his business? He sings in grave-making.

HORATIO: (*Pulling at* HAMLET) Custom hath made it in him a property of easiness.

(HAMLET's *curiosity is growing. He resists* HORATIO's *attempt to walk on. He even takes a step closer to the grave, fighting the stink.*)

HAMLET: 'Tis e'en so. The hand of little employment hath the daintier sense.

(HAMLET *speaks from the royal point of view, yet he is moving ever closer to the grave; dragging the gagging* HORATIO *deeper into the effluvia of the place.*)

(OLD GRAVEDIGGER *begins to heave up skulls from the pit.* HAMLET *stiffens.*)

DIRECTOR: (*Off*) Dja vu: have you been here before? Have you dreamed this before?

OLD GRAVEDIGGER: (*Sings*)
But age with his stealing steps
Hath clawed me in his clutch,

And hath shipped me into the land,
As if I had never been such.

(OLD GRAVEDIGGER *throws up another skull.* HORATIO
turns away, sick. But HAMLET *takes another step closer and
removes the linen rag from his face. He breathes, strained at
first, then almost naturally.*)

(OLD GRAVEDIGGER *still pretends not to see* HAMLET.)

HAMLET: That skull had a tongue in it and could sing
once. How the knave jowls it to the ground as if 'twere
Cain's jawbone, that did the first murder *(Laughs)*
...This might be the pate of a politician which this ass
now o'er-reaches, one that would circumvent God,
might it not?

(HORATIO, *recovering slightly, notes something strange
and new in his prince.*)

HORATIO: ...It might, my lord.

HAMLET: *(Moving closer)* Or of a courtier, which could
say "Good morrow, sweet lord! How dost thou, sweet
lord?" This might be my lord such-a-one that praised
my lord such-a-one's

horse when he meant to beg it, might it not?

(*Something half wild, prophetic in* HAMLET *rivets*
HORATIO. HAMLET'*s grip on his friend's arm is like steel,
now, drawing him ever closer to the pit.*)

HORATIO: Ay, my lord.

HAMLET: *(Closer)* Why, e'en so. And now my Lady
Worm's, chapless and knocked about the mazzard
with a sexton's spade. —Here's fine revolution,
an we had the trick to see it... Did these bones cost
no more the breeding but to play at loggats with them?
Mine ache to think on't.

DIRECTOR: *(Off)* "Revolution"! Horatio's jaw drops.
What's your friend, the Prince, doing here?

(The OLD GRAVEDIGGER *continues to spade and throw skulls over his shoulder, singing all the while.)*

*(*HAMLET *draws closer and closer.* OLD GRAVEDIGGER *sings louder and louder.)*

OLD GRAVEDIGGER: A pickaxe and a spade, a spade,
For and a shrouding sheet,
O, a pit of clay for to be made
For such a guest is meet.

HAMLET: *(Dodging a skull)* —There's another. *(Laughs)*
Why may not that be the skull of a lawyer?

DIRECTOR: *(Off)* Yes! The Prince's mimicry is deadly
accurate, now, he's become a consummate actor and his
royal attitude is melting away in the heat and stench of
the place. —And you, Old Man, turn on the Music Hall.
Now—watch him—more skulls—then watch him
openly!

HAMLET: —A lawyer—where be his quiddities now,
his quillets, his cases, his tenures, and his tricks?
Why does he suffer this mad knave now to knock
him about the sconce with a dirty shovel and will
not tell him of his action of battery? Ha!

*(*HORATIO *is forced to chortle at* HAMLET's *razor staccato, and the sexton does a little jig. The show is on!)*

HAMLET: —Hum, this fellow might be in's time a
great buyer of land, with his statutes, his recognisance,
his fines, his double vouchers, his recoveries. Is this
the fine of his fines and recovery of his recoveries,
to have his fine pate full of fine dirt?

*(*HAMLET *is transformed: he ages, bows, trots, hangs on* HORATIO; *dances a court dance with him; speaks in different accents—his voice an orchestra: he has become "the abstract and brief chronicle" of the death and life of the time of the graveyard.)*

(All the while, HAMLET and the clown mimic and complement each other, and even HORATIO is liberated so far as to pull faces as part of the canvas of characters.)

(Just then, the YOUNG GRAVEDIGGER returns with the stoup of liquor. Of course, the lad, at once, becomes the perfect audience to this inspired improvisation and totentanz.)

HAMLET: —Will his vouchers vouch him no more of his purchases, and double ones too, than the length and breadth of a pair of indentures? The very conveyances of his lands will scarcely lie in this box.

DIRECTOR: *(Off)* Stop dead! Everyone freeze. Hamlet is "The Prince" again. His voice is an ice-pick, now.

HAMLET: ...And must the inheritor himself have no more, ha?

(Silence. HORATIO takes HAMLET's arm, preparing to rejoin the world of the old revenge plot. OLD GRAVEDIGGER uncorks the liquor and takes a swig. All eyes on the prince.)

HORATIO: Not a jot more, my lord.

HAMLET: *(Pause)* ...Is not parchment made of sheepskins?

HORATIO: *(Very carefully)* Ay, my lord, and of calves' skin too.

DIRECTOR: *(Off)* Old Man—don't let him get away— you and your boy need him to live. Life or death! Hamlet or Fortinbras. Hold the bottle up to him. Hold his eye.

HAMLET: They are sheep and calves which seek out assurance in that... I will speak to this fellow. —Whose grave's this, sirrah?

OLD GRAVEDIGGER: *(Pause, drinks)* Mine, sir.

(OLD GRAVEDIGGER , *still pretending not to know who the prince is, passes the liquor to his son for a nip, then they both begin to sing—watching* HAMLET.*)*

OLD & YOUNG GRAVEDIGGERS:
O, a pit of clay for to be made
For such a guest is meet ...

DIRECTOR: *(Off)* The Old Man—that face—do you know him from some past life?

HAMLET: ...I think it be thine indeed, for thou liest in't.

(The sun is setting. A red glow bathes the scene. The old clown squints up from the grave at the prince.)

OLD GRAVEDIGGER: You lie out on't, sir, and therefore 'tis not yours. For my part, I do not lie in't, yet it is mine.

HAMLET: *(A soft laugh)* Thou does lie in't, to be in't and say it is thine. 'Tis for the dead, not for the quick; therefore thou liest.

OLD GRAVEDIGGER: *(Shades his eyes)* 'Tis a quick lie, sir; 'twill away again from me to you.

DIRECTOR: *(Off)* This Clown is too quick to be a "clown". Sink to one knee. Study that face.

HAMLET: ...What man dost thou dig it for?

OLD GRAVEDIGGER: For no man, sir.

HAMLET: *(Reacts)* What woman then?

OLD GRAVEDIGGER: For none, neither.

DIRECTOR: *(Off)* Something's hidden here, some riddle, some enigma; literally under the Prince's nose. Concentrate your powers. Your genius.

HAMLET: Who is't to be buried in't?

OLD GRAVEDIGGER: *(Nose to nose)* One that was a woman, sir, but, rest her soul, she's dead.

(If HAMLET *had begun to half imagine that he was peering into his own grave, now* OPHELIA *fills his being. He draws back, still on one knee, and looks to* HORATIO.)

HAMLET: How absolute the knave is! We must speak by the card or... How long hast thou been a grave-maker?

OLD GRAVEDIGGER: Of all the days i' th' year, I came to't that day our last King Hamlet overcame Norway.

HAMLET: *(Taken aback, tests the clown)* ...How long is that since?

DIRECTOR: *(Off)* Music Hall!

OLD GRAVEDIGGER: Cannot you tell that? Every fool can tell that. It was that very day that young Hamlet was born—he that is mad, and sent into England.

HAMLET: *(Searching)* ...Ay, marry...why was he sent into England?

OLD GRAVEDIGGER: *(Great solemnity)* Why, because he was mad. He shall recover his wits there. Or if he do not, 'tis no great matter there.

HAMLET: *(Caught)* Why?

OLD GRAVEDIGGER: 'Twill not be seen in him there. There the men are as mad as he.

(Nose to nose: "As mad as he (he-he-ha)". The laugh explodes in HAMLET's *face but he does not back up, he presses:)*

HAMLET: How came he mad?

OLD GRAVEDIGGER: *(Solemn again)* Very strangely, they say.

HAMLET: *(Grabbing)* How "strangely"?

OLD GRAVEDIGGER: Faith, e'en with losing his wits!

(Another explosion: "his wits-s-s-s?" HORATIO *is becoming alarmed,* HAMLET *brushes him back. Rounds on the sexton.)*

HAMLET: Upon what ground?

OLD GRAVEDIGGER: Why, here in Denmark
(k—k—k—k!...) I have been Sexton here, man and boy,
thirty years.

DIRECTOR: *(Off)* The last rays of the sun. The Prince
almost touches the Old Man's face. You know it; you
remember, but can't remember. But you will. Close
your eyes— "about my brain..." Do the math: "man
and boy"; "the day Young Hamlet was born"; "thirty
years"; ... "was born" —his birthday, and today—
his death day!

*(In the silence, OLD GRAVEDIGGER sips from the liquor and,
then, passes the stoup to HAMLET. Before HORATIO can
push the potent potion away, HAMLET has taken it and
drunk...)*

DIRECTOR: *(Off)* ...The drink hits you. Good. They're
watching.... Something deep coming—play the King's—
play your father's tomb—up right, where the cross is...
Touch it... Look...There's your "Ghost" —in "compleat
steel" ...What's that? A red ant moving across the
marble? ...And, look, there: it's a, ah, a freckle of green
moss, already, on the statue's helmet. Should you pull
it off? No—no, let it be... Summer's coming... "Rest, rest,
perturbèd spirit" ...O K.

ACTOR: (HAMLET) Wait...

(DIRECTOR comes on stage, slowly to face the problem.)

DIRECTOR: ...Talk to me.

ACTOR: (HAMLET) Let me try it the—let me scrape off
the moss and then—

DIRECTOR: Hamlet's buried his—

ACTOR: (HAMLET) He's not "Hamlet" yet, he's still the—

DIRECTOR: He's buried his father; he's Hamlet at last.

ACTOR: (HAMLET) Not yet.

(Pause. DIRECTOR *acts out what he wants from the actor.*)

DIRECTOR: Right! You have to give us that moment!
...Look: you reach for the moss, to clean it off: "if I
wanted to be free what would I do?" You touch the
cold marble. You shiver with fear. You flinch your hand
away. You feel sick again—like before—then rage—
because *you're sick of being sick!* And you turn and face
all of them—the living and the dead—and you say the
Magic Words: "how long will my father lie in the earth
before he rots?" And it's over. The Ghost is laid. The
King's dead, the Prince dies! Hamlet lives! Full stop.

(Silence. They stare at each other.)

ACTOR: (HAMLET) ...I want to try it one beat later....
He scrapes off the moss, he feels it on his fingers.
And he's trapped again—inside the prince's body.

DIRECTOR: So, he—

ACTOR: (HAMLET) He needs help. He needs an answer.
And that's why he turns to the old man to pose the
hidden question: "if I kill the Prince of Denmark—
will I have to die, too?"

(Silence. They stare. Other actors in wings watching.
Finally:)

DIRECTOR: ...Try it. (He stays on stage to watch.)

(HAMLET resumes the action. Again, he sees the ant
crawling, the moss growing. He stares at the growth on
his father's marble body.)

(HAMLET scrapes it off. Rubs the moss between his fingers,
looks at the residue on his hands. Leans against the tomb,
breathes, slumps—then rushes away, turning to OLD
GRAVEDIGGER.)

HAMLET: How long will a man lie i'th' earth ere he rot?

(Pause. DIRECTOR *speaks then retires to his table,
in darkness.)*

DIRECTOR: ...You're right...I was—you're right.

*(*DIRECTOR *returns to his table.* HAMLET *repeats the
compleat moment.)*

HAMLET: How long will a man lie i'th' earth ere he rot?

OLD GRAVEDIGGER: Faith...if he be not rotten before he
die—as we have many pocky corses nowadays, that
will scarce hold the laying in—he will last you some
eight year or nine year. A tanner will last you nine year.

*(*HAMLET *listens, hears, feels, comprehends. The
*GRAVEDIGGERS *lean against the walls of the pit and
watch the two young men. The sun is going down. The
prince is off balance. No other person in this Elsinore has ever
outwitted him. Never. Until today)*

HAMLET: ...Why he more than another?

DIRECTOR: *(Off, to the* OLD GRAVEDIGGER*)* ...Bring
Hamlet back, now, he's hooked, bring him in. Wait
for the penny to drop.

OLD GRAVEDIGGER: Why, sir, his hide is so tanned with
his trade that he will keep out water a great while; and
your water is a sore decayer of your whoreson dead
body... *(He digs deep—gives a laugh—turns up an old caked
skull.)* ...Here's a skull now hath lien you i' th' earth
three-and-twenty years. *(He picks up the skull with
studied ease, his eyes never leaving the prince's face. Slowly,
like a conjuror, he uses the death's-head to lure* HAMLET *back
down to the open grave.)*

*(The death's-head, of course, is covered with clay, plant life,
and worms. Thus,* HAMLET *jerks back when the old man
holds the reeking thing close to the prince's face.)*

HAMLET: ...Whose was it?

OLD GRAVEDIGGER: *(A laugh)* A whoreson mad fellow's it was. *(Closer)* Whose do you think it was? *(Closer)*

HAMLET: ...Nay, I know not.

OLD GRAVEDIGGER: *(Watching* HAMLET *only)* A pestilence on him for a mad rogue! He poured a flagon of Rhenish on my head once. *(Closer)* This same skull, sir, was, sir—Yorick's skull! —The King's jester.

HAMLET: ...*This?*

OLD GRAVEDIGGER: ...E'en that...

*(*HAMLET *is breathless. Yorick! Of course! From the moment he saw and heard this old clown, he had had an uncanny infection or eruption of an old memory—long forgotten yet, somehow, the ineluctable quintessence of his very being. And* OLD GRAVEDIGGER *had been riddling with him all along.)*

*(*HAMLET, *now, leans closer and closer to the skull; looks from* OLD GRAVEDIGGER's *face to the jester's skull. Back and forth)*

*(*OLD GRAVEDIGGER *moves the skull slowly around the* HAMLET's *face.)*

HAMLET: *(Panting)* Let me see it ...

*(*OLD GRAVEDIGGER *moves the skull closer, then, suddenly slips the ghastly bones into* HAMLET's *hand.)*

*(*HAMLETt *is frozen with atavistic terror.* HORATIO, *as well. The two clowns lean forward, flanking the prince.)*

*(*HAMLET *slowly directs his head to swivel back to look at the thing clutched in his claw. To look, to breathe, and to come to grips with the thing—worms, moss and all. The prince looks, pants, then breathes...)*

DIRECTOR: *(Off)* ...You were right. This is where it appears. The nausea passes. The skull reeks but something else is rising in him. He is *re-membering.* His

entire body is breaking out in memory... Something
rising... Look at the Old Clown, then back to Yorick,
then back—and, then, suddenly, he knows what's
possessing him: love. Old love... So, you were right.

HAMLET: Alas, poor Yorick! I knew him, Horatio—
a fellow of infinite jest, of most excellent fancy.
*(He slowly cleans the skull of the dirt, moss, worms.
He uses his handkerchief and his fingers.)*

*(GRAVEDIGGERS smile and nod. HORATIO gapes.
HAMLET's eyes are locked on OLD GRAVEDIGGER's face.)*

HAMLET: He hath borne me on his back a thousand
times...and now how abhorred in my imagination it is!
My gorge rises at it.... Here hung those lips that I have
kissed I know not how oft.... Where be your gibes now?
Your gambols? Your songs? *(He hums a remembered tune:
Imperious Caesar)* Your flashes of merriment that were
wont to set the table on a roar? Not one now to mock
your own grinning? Quite chapfallen? ...Now get you
to my lady's chamber, and tell her, let her paint an inch
thick, to this favour she must come. Make her laugh at
that.

*(HAMLET studies the "clean" skull, before slowly handing it
back to the sexton. The old man gives it a final wipe and sets
it on the lip of the grave.)*

*(OLD GRAVEDIGGER, then, heaves himself up and sits next
to HAMLET, graveside; and the young sexton, his son, joins
them. They pass the liquor. Birdsong. HAMLET insists that
HORATIO take a sip of the brew. HORATIO, at last, wipes the
mouth of the container and tastes the mixture. They all laugh
at his grimace, and he sits down, too.)*

HAMLET: ...Prithee, Horatio, tell me one thing.

HORATIO: What's that, my lord?

HAMLET: Dost thou think Alexander looked o' this
fashion i' th' earth?

HORATIO: ...E'en so.

HAMLET: And smelt so? Pah!

HORATIO: E'en so, my lord.

(YOUNG GRAVEDIGGER *is now asleep on* OLD
GRAVEDIGGER*'s shoulder. The faces of the four are
lit by the last rays of the sun.*)

HAMLET: ...To what base uses we may return, Horatio!
Why may not imagination trace the noble dust of
"Alexander" till he find it stopping a bunghole?

(OLD GRAVEDIGGER *winks and nods at* HAMLET. YOUNG
GRAVEDIGGER *snores.* HORATIO *gasps.*)

HORATIO: 'Twere to consider too curiously to consider
so.

(HORATIO *may not have the "trick" to see the "fine
revolution" in* HAMLET*'s words, but the old clown not only
sees it, he says it—to himself—just as if he had written the
prince's part.*)

HAMLET: No, faith, not a jot: but to follow him thither,
with modesty enough and likelihood to lead it—as
thus: Alexander died, Alexander was buried, Alexander
returneth to dust; the dust is earth, of earth we make
loam; and why of that loam whereto he was converted
might they not stop—a beer barrel?

(*And* HAMLET *picks up the skull and tosses it to* OLD
GRAVEDIGGER. *That ancient gentleman looks at it,
spits on it—in order to give the thing a final polish with
his sleeve,—plants a farewell kiss on the cranium, and
tosses it back to* HAMLET.)

(HAMLET *and* OLD GRAVEDIGGER *chuckle to each other
as if to say, "Whose skull was this, really—and what
difference does it make?"*)

(*Then* HAMLET *kisses it goodbye and lofts it back into the
grave. He lifts the stoup of liquor in a toast to the departed;*

*the sexton offers his toast, too. And it is over: he has buried
his father. He is quietly joyful, for the first time.)*

*(*YOUNG GRAVEDIGGER *snores on his father's shoulder.
And* HORATIO? *He sleeps softly on* HAMLET's. *The prince
and the clown look down into the grave. The grave—of
Yorick, and Alexander, and Julius Caesar, let alone Hamlet
Senior and his infernal ghost—of all the interchangeable
heroes and fools in the long weary increment since Genesis.)*

*(The play is at an end, at last. All that remains is for the
prince and the old jester to sing one last song. So that
Alexander and Julius Caesar; and the "perturbed spirits"
of the two fathers—the false King Hamlet, and the true fool,
Yorick—can rest in peace until the end of this day; when the
old cown will bury yung* HAMLET *with all the others that
he had loved and lost.)*

HAMLET: & OLD GRAVEDIGGER: *(Sing)*
Imperious Caesar, dead and turned to clay,
Might stop a hole to keep the wind away.
O, that that earth which kept the world in awe
Should patch a wall t'expel the winter's flaw!

(The prince and the clown sing Yorick's Song. *The other
two sleep. The sun's last rays are fading. The song ends.
Silence. The actors wait.)*

(From the dark theatre, the DIRECTOR's *voice, as he and*
STAGE MANAGER, *arm in arm, walk on stage.)*

DIRECTOR: ...Yeah... Stop a "Bunghole" —patch a
"beer barrel". Yeah... Well... Shall we sing "Yorick's
Song" one more time? And then go home. Annnnd
thennnn—tomorrow—we'll pick up with Ophelia's
funeral procession to the cemetery—annnnd the
g'damn Revenge Plot! *(To the* HAMLET *actor)* ...You
were spot on: he's free at last—and forever...

(And the six of them—joined by the others—sing Yorick's
Song, *again.)*

ALL: Imperious Caesar, dead and turned to clay,
Might stop a hole to keep the wind away.
O, that that earth which kept the world in awe
Should patch a wall t'expel the winter's flaw!

(At the curtain call the entire cast come on singing Yorick's
Song.*)*

*(The tempo is syncopated and the actors dance a jig as they
sing—endeavouring to inspire the audience to join them in*
Yorick's Song*).*

END OF PLAY

www.ingramcontent.com/pod-product-compliance
Lightning Source LLC
Chambersburg PA
CBHW070022110426
42741CB00034B/2297